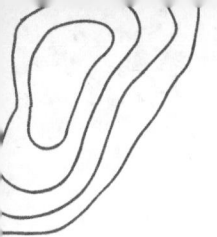

5-MINUTE MORNING JOURNAL

THIS PLANNER BELONGS TO:

_____

WWW.THE JOURNALBOX.COM

sales@thejournalbox.com | 215-298-9475

The Journal Box is a Woman, Minority, and Veteran Owned Company.

@2021 - The Journal Box

ISBN 978-1-4357-6531-3

"Each morning we are born again. What we do today is what matters most."
~ Buddha

MORNING HABITS
OF SUCCESSFUL PEOPLE

Write down little tasks in the morning to clear your head

Start the day with a good sweat

Ask yourself if it will matter in a day, week, month or year

See the potential in others

Practice self-care and mindfulness

Ask yourself if it will matter in a day, week, month or year

See the potential in others

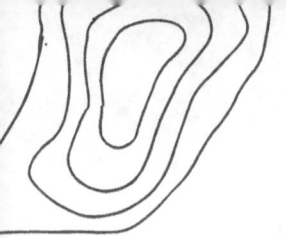

GOOD MORNING!!

___/___/___

M T W T F S S
○ ○ ○ ○ ○ ○ ○

TODAY'S APPOINTMENTS

6:00	7:00	8:00	9:00	10:00	11:00	12:00 PM	1:00	2:00	3:00	4:00	5:00	6:00

TO DO LIST

MY MOODS

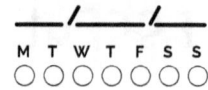

TO DO LIST

FOR TOMORROW

HEALTH & FITNESS

QUICK NOTE

WATER INTAKE

TODAY'S NOTES

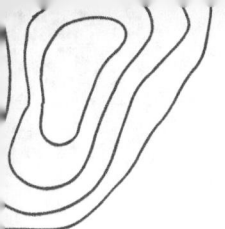
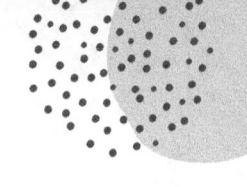

GOOD MORNING!!

___/___/___

M T W T F S S
○ ○ ○ ○ ○ ○ ○

TODAY'S APPOINTMENTS

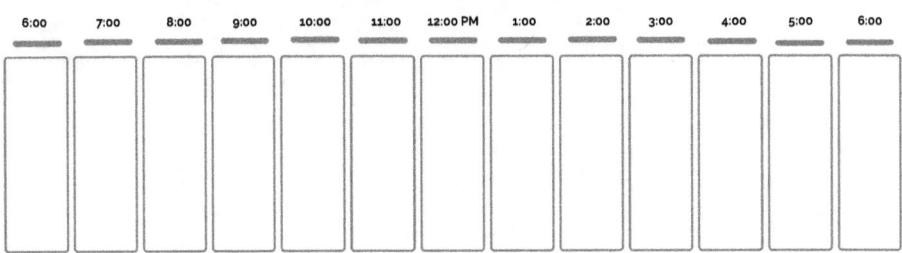

6:00	7:00	8:00	9:00	10:00	11:00	12:00 PM	1:00	2:00	3:00	4:00	5:00	6:00

TO DO LIST

MY MOODS

FOR TOMORROW

QUICK NOTE

TO DO LIST

HEALTH & FITNESS

WATER INTAKE

TODAY'S NOTES

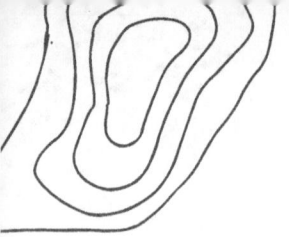

GOOD MORNING!!

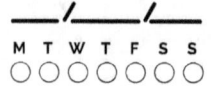

___ / ___ / ___

M T W T F S S
○ ○ ○ ○ ○ ○ ○

TODAY'S APPOINTMENTS

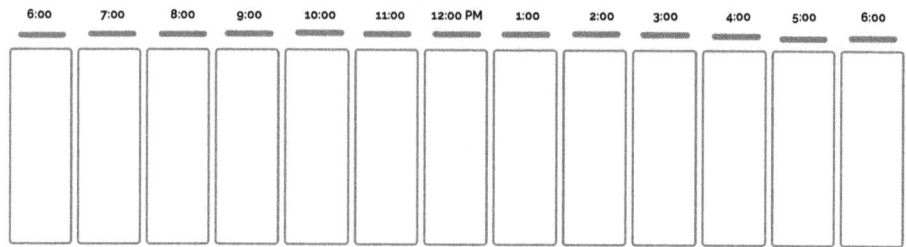

6:00	7:00	8:00	9:00	10:00	11:00	12:00 PM	1:00	2:00	3:00	4:00	5:00	6:00

TO DO LIST

MY MOODS

FOR TOMORROW

QUICK NOTE

TO DO LIST

WATER INTAKE

HEALTH & FITNESS

TODAY'S NOTES

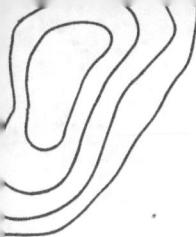

GOOD MORNING!!

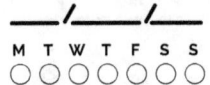

M T W T F S S
○ ○ ○ ○ ○ ○ ○

TODAY'S APPOINTMENTS

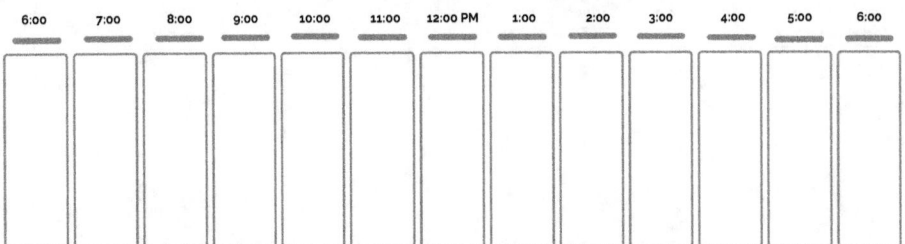

6:00	7:00	8:00	9:00	10:00	11:00	12:00 PM	1:00	2:00	3:00	4:00	5:00	6:00

TO DO LIST

MY MOODS

FOR TOMORROW

QUICK NOTE

TO DO LIST

HEALTH & FITNESS

WATER INTAKE

TODAY'S NOTES

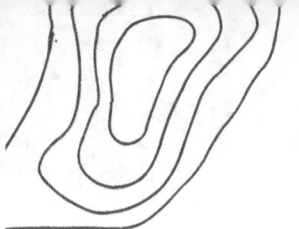

GooD MorNING!!

___ / ___ / ___

M T W T F S S
◯ ◯ ◯ ◯ ◯ ◯ ◯

TODAY'S APPOINTMENTS

6:00	7:00	8:00	9:00	10:00	11:00	12:00 PM	1:00	2:00	3:00	4:00	5:00	6:00

TO DO LIST

MY MOODS

FOR TOMORROW

QUICK NOTE

TO DO LIST

HEALTH & FITNESS

WATER INTAKE

TODAY'S NOTES

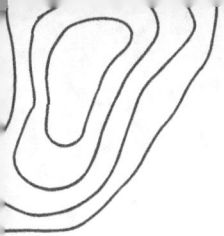

GOOD MORNING!!

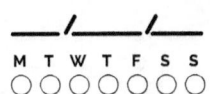

M T W T F S S
○ ○ ○ ○ ○ ○ ○

TODAY'S APPOINTMENTS

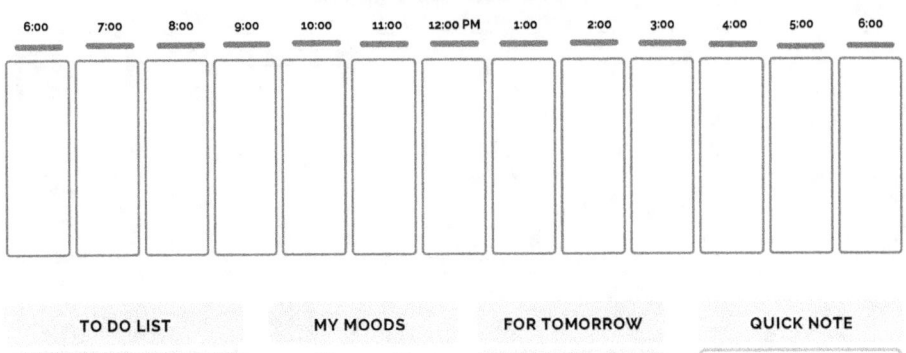

6:00	7:00	8:00	9:00	10:00	11:00	12:00 PM	1:00	2:00	3:00	4:00	5:00	6:00

TO DO LIST

MY MOODS

FOR TOMORROW

QUICK NOTE

TO DO LIST

HEALTH & FITNESS

WATER INTAKE

TODAY'S NOTES

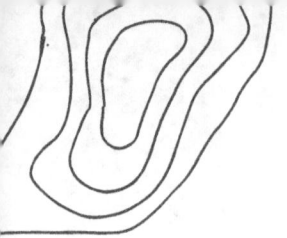

GOOD MORNING!!

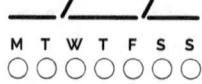

M T W T F S S
○ ○ ○ ○ ○ ○ ○

TODAY'S APPOINTMENTS

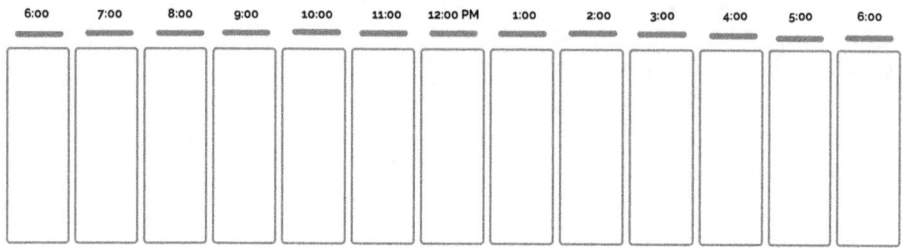

6:00	7:00	8:00	9:00	10:00	11:00	12:00 PM	1:00	2:00	3:00	4:00	5:00	6:00

TO DO LIST

MY MOODS

FOR TOMORROW

QUICK NOTE

TO DO LIST

HEALTH & FITNESS

WATER INTAKE

TODAY'S NOTES

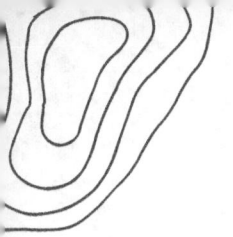

GOOD MORNING!!

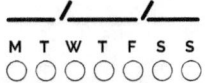

M T W T F S S
○ ○ ○ ○ ○ ○ ○

TODAY'S APPOINTMENTS

6:00	7:00	8:00	9:00	10:00	11:00	12:00 PM	1:00	2:00	3:00	4:00	5:00	6:00

TO DO LIST	MY MOODS	FOR TOMORROW	QUICK NOTE

TO DO LIST

HEALTH & FITNESS

WATER INTAKE

TODAY'S NOTES

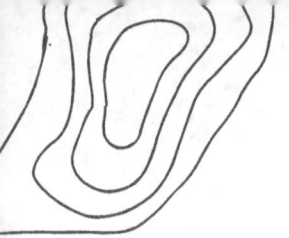

GOOD MORNING!!

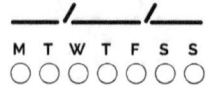

M T W T F S S
○ ○ ○ ○ ○ ○ ○

TODAY'S APPOINTMENTS

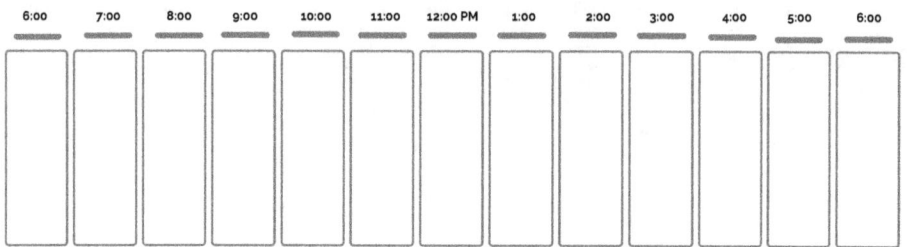

6:00	7:00	8:00	9:00	10:00	11:00	12:00 PM	1:00	2:00	3:00	4:00	5:00	6:00

TO DO LIST

MY MOODS

FOR TOMORROW

QUICK NOTE

TO DO LIST

HEALTH & FITNESS

WATER INTAKE

TODAY'S NOTES

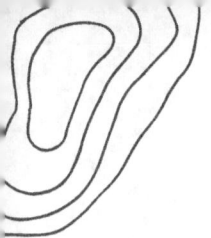
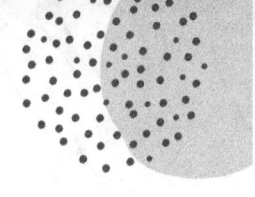

GOOD MORNING!!

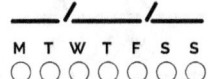

M T W T F S S
○ ○ ○ ○ ○ ○ ○

TODAY'S APPOINTMENTS

6:00	7:00	8:00	9:00	10:00	11:00	12:00 PM	1:00	2:00	3:00	4:00	5:00	6:00

TO DO LIST

MY MOODS

FOR TOMORROW

QUICK NOTE

TO DO LIST

HEALTH & FITNESS

WATER INTAKE

TODAY'S NOTES

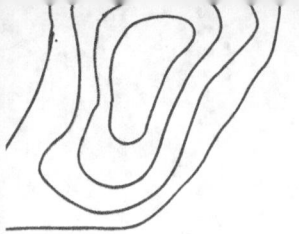

GOOD MORNING!!

___/___/___

M T W T F S S
○ ○ ○ ○ ○ ○ ○

TODAY'S APPOINTMENTS

6:00	7:00	8:00	9:00	10:00	11:00	12:00 PM	1:00	2:00	3:00	4:00	5:00	6:00

TO DO LIST

MY MOODS

FOR TOMORROW

QUICK NOTE

TO DO LIST

HEALTH & FITNESS

WATER INTAKE

TODAY'S NOTES

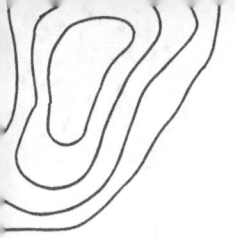

GOOD MORNING!!

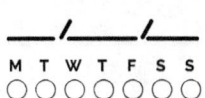

M T W T F S S
○ ○ ○ ○ ○ ○ ○

TODAY'S APPOINTMENTS

6:00	7:00	8:00	9:00	10:00	11:00	12:00 PM	1:00	2:00	3:00	4:00	5:00	6:00

TO DO LIST

MY MOODS

FOR TOMORROW

QUICK NOTE

WATER INTAKE

TO DO LIST

HEALTH & FITNESS

TODAY'S NOTES

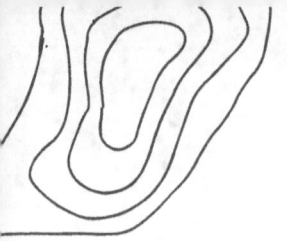

GOOD MORNING!!

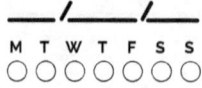

M T W T F S S
◯ ◯ ◯ ◯ ◯ ◯ ◯

TODAY'S APPOINTMENTS

6:00	7:00	8:00	9:00	10:00	11:00	12:00 PM	1:00	2:00	3:00	4:00	5:00	6:00

TO DO LIST

MY MOODS

FOR TOMORROW

QUICK NOTE

TO DO LIST

WATER INTAKE

HEALTH & FITNESS

TODAY'S NOTES

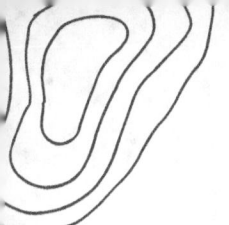
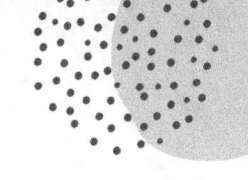

GOOD MORNING!!

___/___/___

M T W T F S S
○ ○ ○ ○ ○ ○ ○

TODAY'S APPOINTMENTS

6:00	7:00	8:00	9:00	10:00	11:00	12:00 PM	1:00	2:00	3:00	4:00	5:00	6:00

TO DO LIST

MY MOODS

FOR TOMORROW

QUICK NOTE

TO DO LIST

WATER INTAKE

HEALTH & FITNESS

TODAY'S NOTES

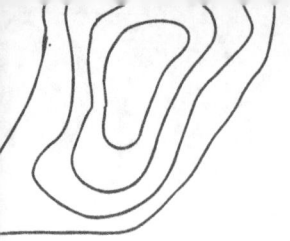

GOOD MORNING!!

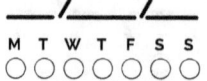

M T W T F S S
○ ○ ○ ○ ○ ○ ○

TODAY'S APPOINTMENTS

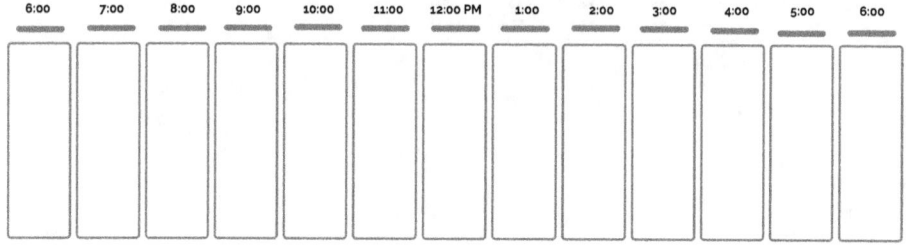

6:00	7:00	8:00	9:00	10:00	11:00	12:00 PM	1:00	2:00	3:00	4:00	5:00	6:00

TO DO LIST

MY MOODS

FOR TOMORROW

QUICK NOTE

TO DO LIST

HEALTH & FITNESS

WATER INTAKE

TODAY'S NOTES

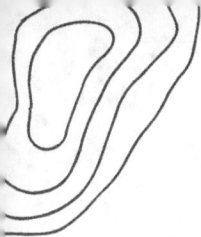
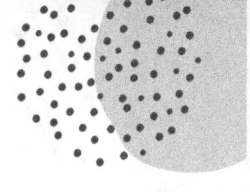

GOOD MORNING!!

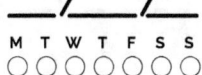

M T W T F S S
○ ○ ○ ○ ○ ○ ○

TODAY'S APPOINTMENTS

6:00	7:00	8:00	9:00	10:00	11:00	12:00 PM	1:00	2:00	3:00	4:00	5:00	6:00

TO DO LIST

MY MOODS

FOR TOMORROW

QUICK NOTE

TO DO LIST

WATER INTAKE

HEALTH & FITNESS

TODAY'S NOTES

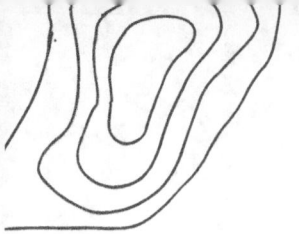

GOOD MORNING!!

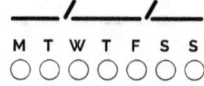

M T W T F S S
○ ○ ○ ○ ○ ○ ○

TODAY'S APPOINTMENTS

6:00	7:00	8:00	9:00	10:00	11:00	12:00 PM	1:00	2:00	3:00	4:00	5:00	6:00

TO DO LIST

MY MOODS

FOR TOMORROW

QUICK NOTE

TO DO LIST

HEALTH & FITNESS

WATER INTAKE

TODAY'S NOTES

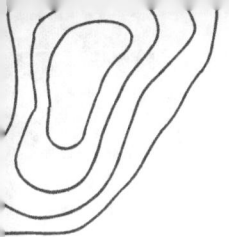
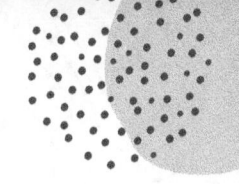

GOOD MORNING!!

___/___/___

M T W T F S S
○ ○ ○ ○ ○ ○ ○

TODAY'S APPOINTMENTS

6:00	7:00	8:00	9:00	10:00	11:00	12:00 PM	1:00	2:00	3:00	4:00	5:00	6:00

TO DO LIST

MY MOODS

FOR TOMORROW

QUICK NOTE

TO DO LIST

WATER INTAKE

HEALTH & FITNESS

TODAY'S NOTES

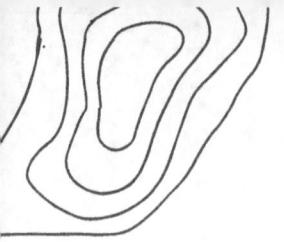

GOOD MORNING!!

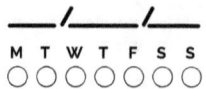

M T W T F S S
○ ○ ○ ○ ○ ○ ○

TODAY'S APPOINTMENTS

6:00	7:00	8:00	9:00	10:00	11:00	12:00 PM	1:00	2:00	3:00	4:00	5:00	6:00

TO DO LIST

MY MOODS

FOR TOMORROW

QUICK NOTE

TO DO LIST

HEALTH & FITNESS

WATER INTAKE

TODAY'S NOTES

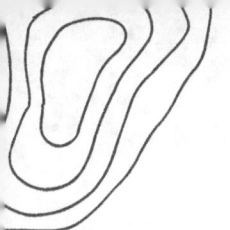
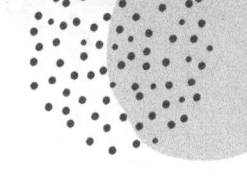

GOOD MORNING!!

___ / ___ / ___

M T W T F S S
○ ○ ○ ○ ○ ○ ○

TODAY'S APPOINTMENTS

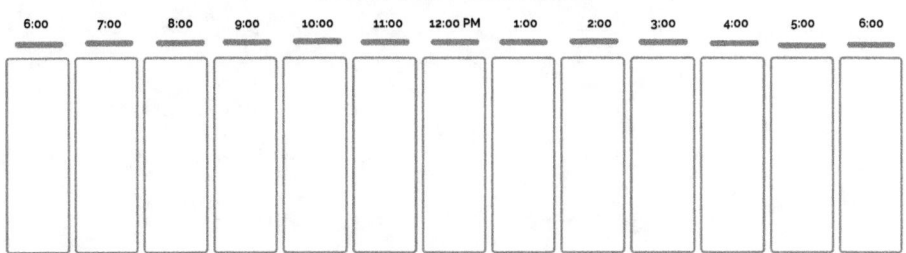

6:00	7:00	8:00	9:00	10:00	11:00	12:00 PM	1:00	2:00	3:00	4:00	5:00	6:00

TO DO LIST

MY MOODS

FOR TOMORROW

QUICK NOTE

TO DO LIST

HEALTH & FITNESS

WATER INTAKE

TODAY'S NOTES

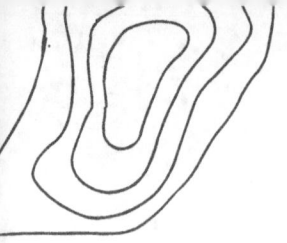

GooD MorNiNG!!

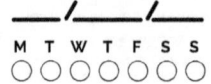

____/____/____

M T W T F S S
○ ○ ○ ○ ○ ○ ○

TODAY'S APPOINTMENTS

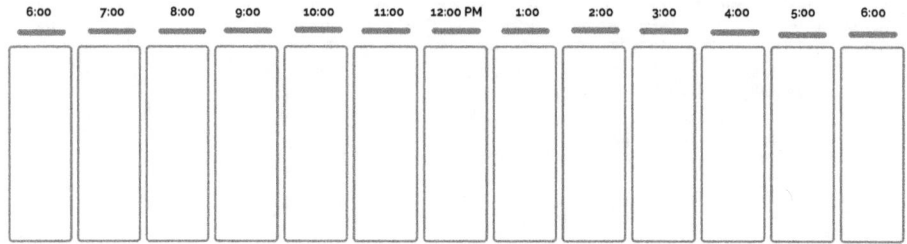

6:00	7:00	8:00	9:00	10:00	11:00	12:00 PM	1:00	2:00	3:00	4:00	5:00	6:00

TO DO LIST

MY MOODS

FOR TOMORROW

QUICK NOTE

TO DO LIST

HEALTH & FITNESS

WATER INTAKE

TODAY'S NOTES

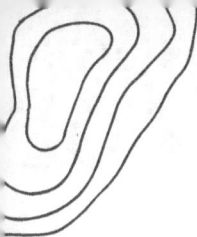

GooD MorNING!!

___/___/___

M T W T F S S
○ ○ ○ ○ ○ ○ ○

TODAY'S APPOINTMENTS

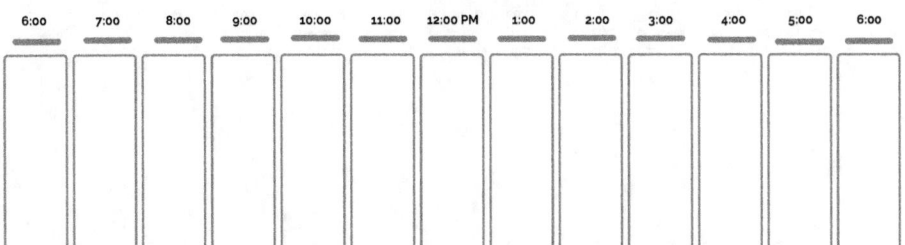

6:00	7:00	8:00	9:00	10:00	11:00	12:00 PM	1:00	2:00	3:00	4:00	5:00	6:00

TO DO LIST

MY MOODS

FOR TOMORROW

QUICK NOTE

TO DO LIST

HEALTH & FITNESS

WATER INTAKE

TODAY'S NOTES

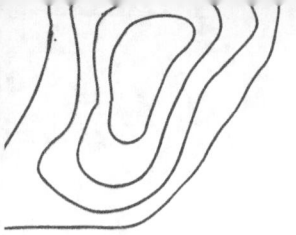

GOOD MORNING!!

___/___/___

M T W T F S S
○ ○ ○ ○ ○ ○ ○

TODAY'S APPOINTMENTS

6:00	7:00	8:00	9:00	10:00	11:00	12:00 PM	1:00	2:00	3:00	4:00	5:00	6:00

TO DO LIST

MY MOODS

FOR TOMORROW

QUICK NOTE

TO DO LIST

HEALTH & FITNESS

WATER INTAKE

TODAY'S NOTES

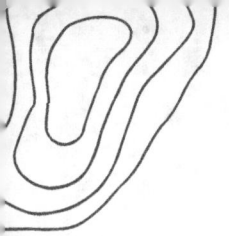

Good Morning!!

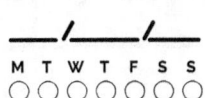

M T W T F S S
○ ○ ○ ○ ○ ○ ○

TODAY'S APPOINTMENTS

6:00	7:00	8:00	9:00	10:00	11:00	12:00 PM	1:00	2:00	3:00	4:00	5:00	6:00

TO DO LIST

MY MOODS

FOR TOMORROW

QUICK NOTE

TO DO LIST

HEALTH & FITNESS

WATER INTAKE

TODAY'S NOTES

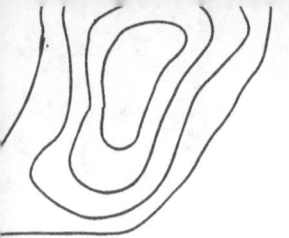

GooD MorNinG!!

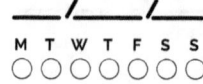

___ / ___ / ___

M T W T F S S
○ ○ ○ ○ ○ ○ ○

TODAY'S APPOINTMENTS

6:00	7:00	8:00	9:00	10:00	11:00	12:00 PM	1:00	2:00	3:00	4:00	5:00	6:00

TO DO LIST

MY MOODS

FOR TOMORROW

QUICK NOTE

TO DO LIST

WATER INTAKE

HEALTH & FITNESS

TODAY'S NOTES

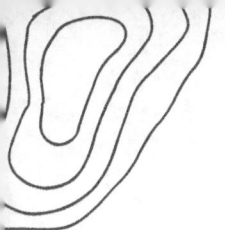

GOOD MORNING!!

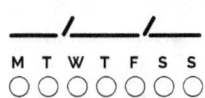

M T W T F S S
○ ○ ○ ○ ○ ○ ○

TODAY'S APPOINTMENTS

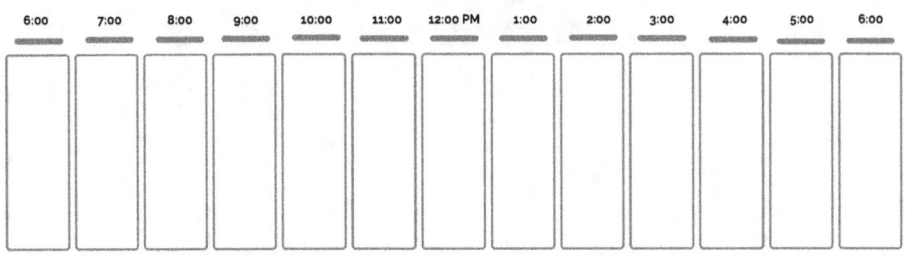

6:00	7:00	8:00	9:00	10:00	11:00	12:00 PM	1:00	2:00	3:00	4:00	5:00	6:00

TO DO LIST

MY MOODS

FOR TOMORROW

QUICK NOTE

TO DO LIST

HEALTH & FITNESS

WATER INTAKE

TODAY'S NOTES

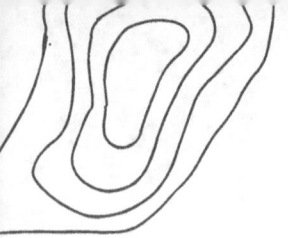

GOOD MORNING!!

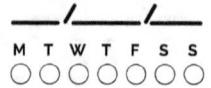

____/____/____

M T W T F S S
○ ○ ○ ○ ○ ○ ○

TODAY'S APPOINTMENTS

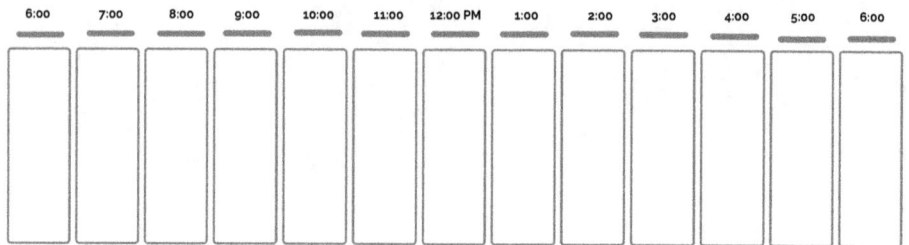

6:00	7:00	8:00	9:00	10:00	11:00	12:00 PM	1:00	2:00	3:00	4:00	5:00	6:00

TO DO LIST

MY MOODS

FOR TOMORROW

QUICK NOTE

WATER INTAKE

TO DO LIST

HEALTH & FITNESS

TODAY'S NOTES

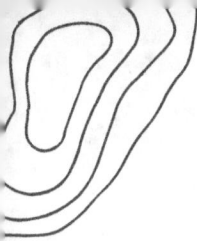

GOOD MORNING!!

____/____/____

M T W T F S S
○ ○ ○ ○ ○ ○ ○

TODAY'S APPOINTMENTS

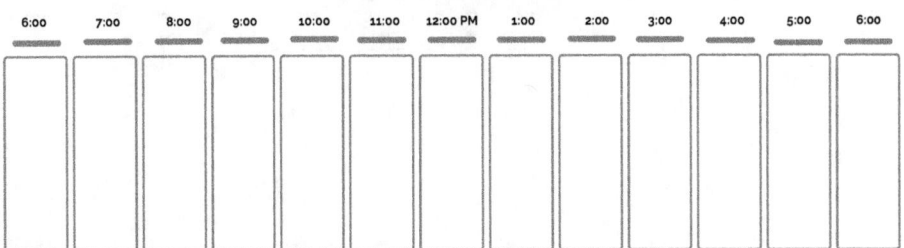

6:00	7:00	8:00	9:00	10:00	11:00	12:00 PM	1:00	2:00	3:00	4:00	5:00	6:00

TO DO LIST

MY MOODS

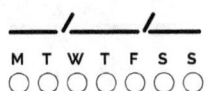

FOR TOMORROW

QUICK NOTE

TO DO LIST

HEALTH & FITNESS

WATER INTAKE

TODAY'S NOTES

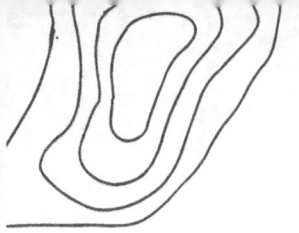

GOOD MORNING!!

___/___/___

M T W T F S S
◯ ◯ ◯ ◯ ◯ ◯ ◯

TODAY'S APPOINTMENTS

6:00	7:00	8:00	9:00	10:00	11:00	12:00 PM	1:00	2:00	3:00	4:00	5:00	6:00

TO DO LIST

MY MOODS

FOR TOMORROW

QUICK NOTE

TO DO LIST

HEALTH & FITNESS

WATER INTAKE

TODAY'S NOTES

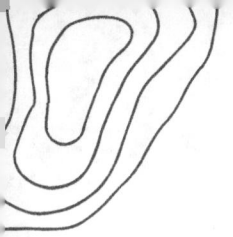

GOOD MORNING!!

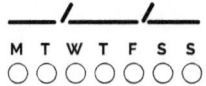

M T W T F S S
○ ○ ○ ○ ○ ○ ○

TODAY'S APPOINTMENTS

6:00	7:00	8:00	9:00	10:00	11:00	12:00 PM	1:00	2:00	3:00	4:00	5:00	6:00

TO DO LIST

MY MOODS

FOR TOMORROW

QUICK NOTE

TO DO LIST

HEALTH & FITNESS

WATER INTAKE

TODAY'S NOTES

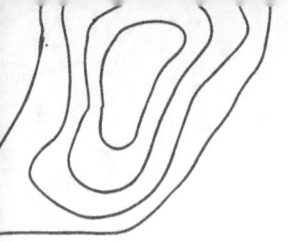

GOOD MORNING!!

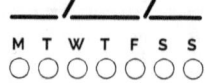

__/__/__

M T W T F S S
○ ○ ○ ○ ○ ○ ○

TODAY'S APPOINTMENTS

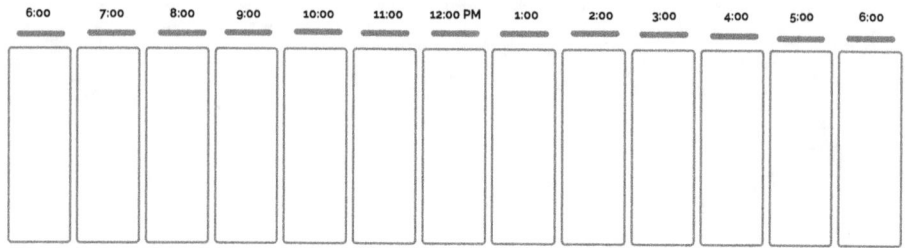

6:00	7:00	8:00	9:00	10:00	11:00	12:00 PM	1:00	2:00	3:00	4:00	5:00	6:00

TO DO LIST

MY MOODS

FOR TOMORROW

QUICK NOTE

TO DO LIST

WATER INTAKE

HEALTH & FITNESS

TODAY'S NOTES

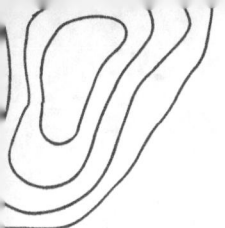

GooD MorNing!!

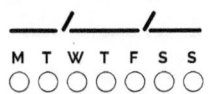

__ / __ / __

M T W T F S S
○ ○ ○ ○ ○ ○ ○

TODAY'S APPOINTMENTS

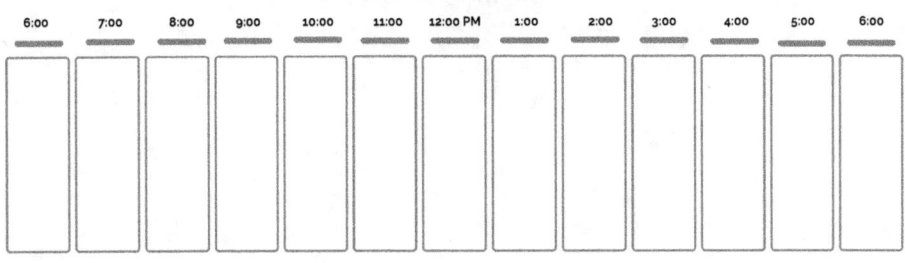

6:00	7:00	8:00	9:00	10:00	11:00	12:00 PM	1:00	2:00	3:00	4:00	5:00	6:00

TO DO LIST

MY MOODS

FOR TOMORROW

QUICK NOTE

TO DO LIST

HEALTH & FITNESS

WATER INTAKE

TODAY'S NOTES

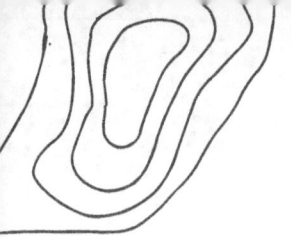

GooD MorninG!!

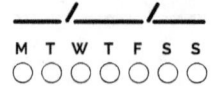

M T W T F S S
○ ○ ○ ○ ○ ○ ○

TODAY'S APPOINTMENTS

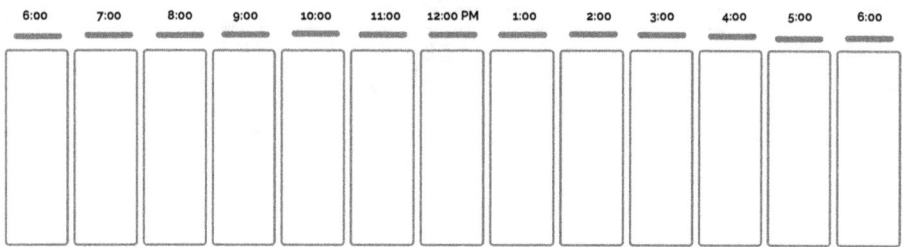

6:00	7:00	8:00	9:00	10:00	11:00	12:00 PM	1:00	2:00	3:00	4:00	5:00	6:00

TO DO LIST

MY MOODS

FOR TOMORROW

QUICK NOTE

TO DO LIST

HEALTH & FITNESS

WATER INTAKE

TODAY'S NOTES

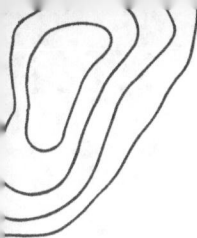
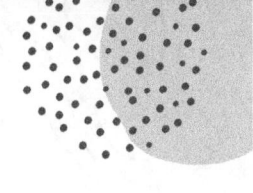

GOOD MORNING!!

___/___/___

M T W T F S S
○ ○ ○ ○ ○ ○ ○

TODAY'S APPOINTMENTS

6:00	7:00	8:00	9:00	10:00	11:00	12:00 PM	1:00	2:00	3:00	4:00	5:00	6:00

TO DO LIST

MY MOODS

FOR TOMORROW

QUICK NOTE

TO DO LIST

HEALTH & FITNESS

WATER INTAKE

TODAY'S NOTES

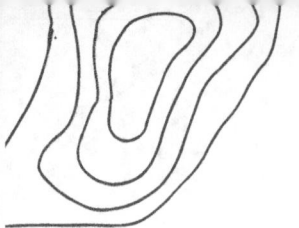

GooD MorNinG!!

__/__/__

M T W T F S S
○ ○ ○ ○ ○ ○ ○

TODAY'S APPOINTMENTS

6:00	7:00	8:00	9:00	10:00	11:00	12:00 PM	1:00	2:00	3:00	4:00	5:00	6:00

TO DO LIST

MY MOODS

FOR TOMORROW

QUICK NOTE

TO DO LIST

WATER INTAKE

HEALTH & FITNESS

TODAY'S NOTES

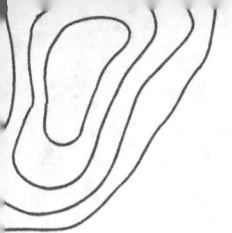

GOOD MORNING!!

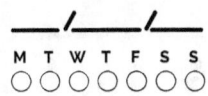

___ / ___ / ___

M T W T F S S
○ ○ ○ ○ ○ ○ ○

TODAY'S APPOINTMENTS

6:00	7:00	8:00	9:00	10:00	11:00	12:00 PM	1:00	2:00	3:00	4:00	5:00	6:00

TO DO LIST

MY MOODS

FOR TOMORROW

QUICK NOTE

TO DO LIST

HEALTH & FITNESS

WATER INTAKE

TODAY'S NOTES

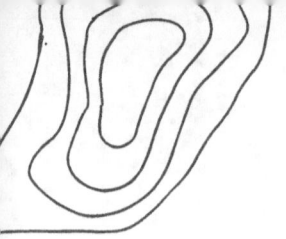

GOOD MORNING!!

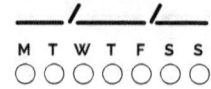

M T W T F S S
○ ○ ○ ○ ○ ○ ○

TODAY'S APPOINTMENTS

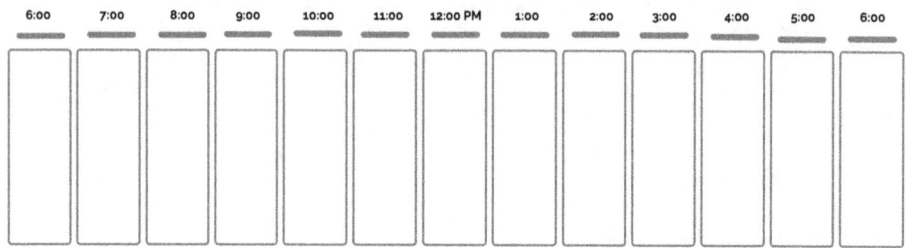

6:00	7:00	8:00	9:00	10:00	11:00	12:00 PM	1:00	2:00	3:00	4:00	5:00	6:00

TO DO LIST

MY MOODS

FOR TOMORROW

QUICK NOTE

TO DO LIST

HEALTH & FITNESS

WATER INTAKE

TODAY'S NOTES

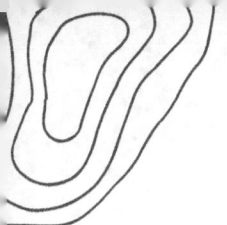

GooD Morning!!

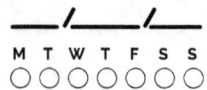

M T W T F S S
○ ○ ○ ○ ○ ○ ○

TODAY'S APPOINTMENTS

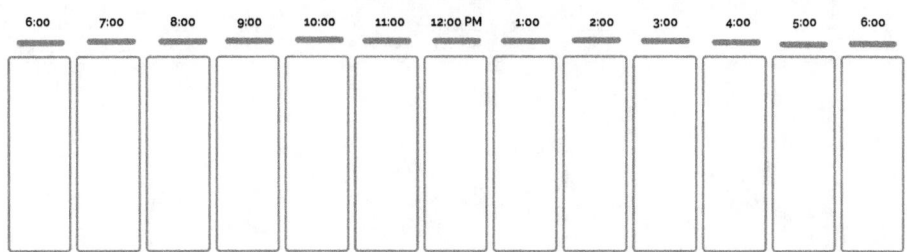

6:00	7:00	8:00	9:00	10:00	11:00	12:00 PM	1:00	2:00	3:00	4:00	5:00	6:00

TO DO LIST

MY MOODS

FOR TOMORROW

QUICK NOTE

TO DO LIST

HEALTH & FITNESS

WATER INTAKE

TODAY'S NOTES

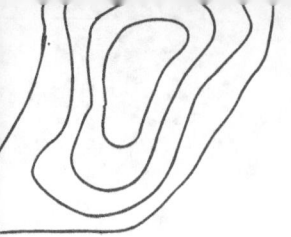

GOOD MORNING!!

___/___/___

M T W T F S S
○ ○ ○ ○ ○ ○ ○

TODAY'S APPOINTMENTS

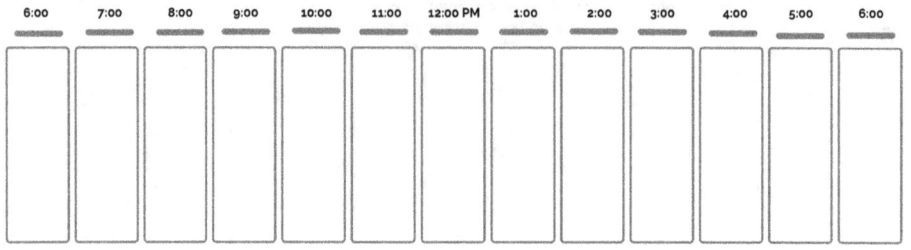

6:00	7:00	8:00	9:00	10:00	11:00	12:00 PM	1:00	2:00	3:00	4:00	5:00	6:00

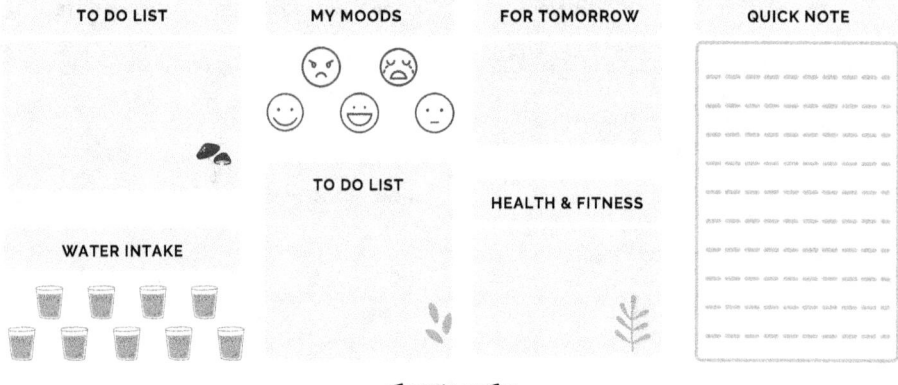

TO DO LIST

MY MOODS

FOR TOMORROW

QUICK NOTE

TO DO LIST

HEALTH & FITNESS

WATER INTAKE

TODAY'S NOTES

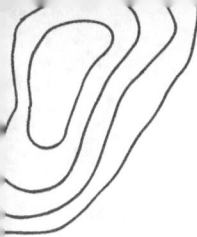

GOOD MORNING!!

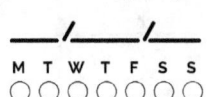

M T W T F S S
○ ○ ○ ○ ○ ○ ○

TODAY'S APPOINTMENTS

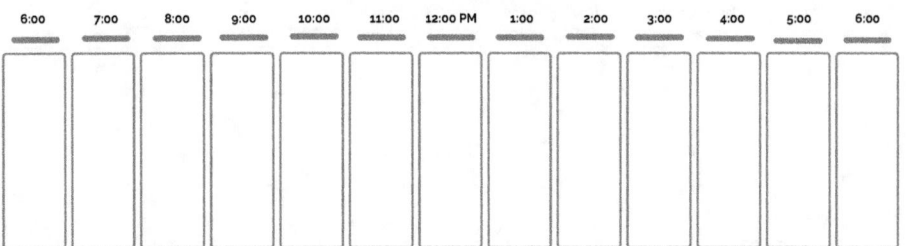

6:00	7:00	8:00	9:00	10:00	11:00	12:00 PM	1:00	2:00	3:00	4:00	5:00	6:00

TO DO LIST

MY MOODS

FOR TOMORROW

QUICK NOTE

WATER INTAKE

TO DO LIST

HEALTH & FITNESS

TODAY'S NOTES

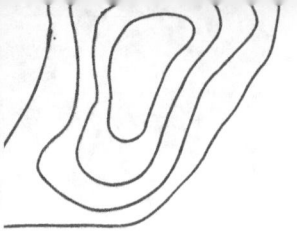

GOOD MORNING!!

___ / ___ / ___

M T W T F S S
○ ○ ○ ○ ○ ○ ○

TODAY'S APPOINTMENTS

6:00	7:00	8:00	9:00	10:00	11:00	12:00 PM	1:00	2:00	3:00	4:00	5:00	6:00

TO DO LIST

MY MOODS

FOR TOMORROW

QUICK NOTE

TO DO LIST

HEALTH & FITNESS

WATER INTAKE

TODAY'S NOTES

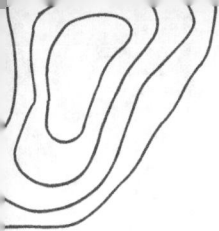

GOOD MORNING!!

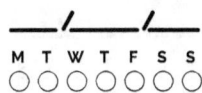

M T W T F S S
◯ ◯ ◯ ◯ ◯ ◯ ◯

TODAY'S APPOINTMENTS

6:00	7:00	8:00	9:00	10:00	11:00	12:00 PM	1:00	2:00	3:00	4:00	5:00	6:00

TO DO LIST

MY MOODS

FOR TOMORROW

QUICK NOTE

TO DO LIST

HEALTH & FITNESS

WATER INTAKE

TODAY'S NOTES

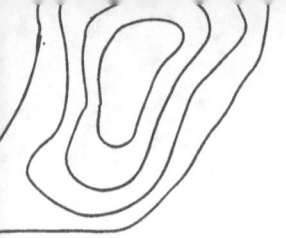

GOOD MORNING!!

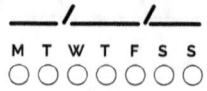

M T W T F S S
◯ ◯ ◯ ◯ ◯ ◯ ◯

TODAY'S APPOINTMENTS

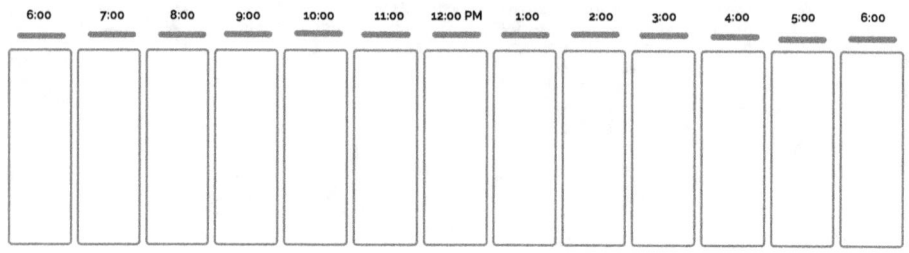

6:00	7:00	8:00	9:00	10:00	11:00	12:00 PM	1:00	2:00	3:00	4:00	5:00	6:00

TO DO LIST

MY MOODS

FOR TOMORROW

QUICK NOTE

TO DO LIST

HEALTH & FITNESS

WATER INTAKE

TODAY'S NOTES

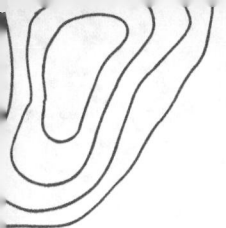

GOOD MORNING!!

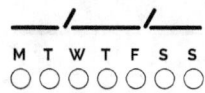

M T W T F S S
◯ ◯ ◯ ◯ ◯ ◯ ◯

TODAY'S APPOINTMENTS

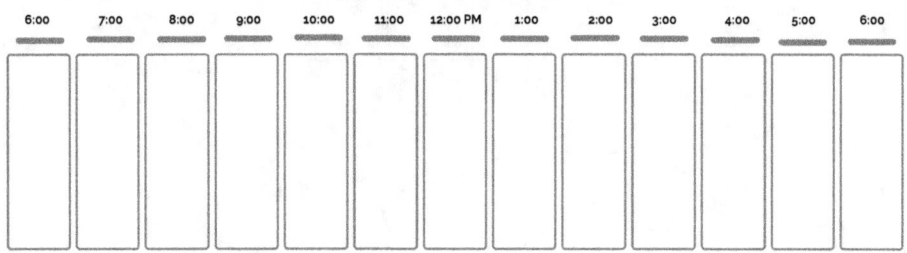

| 6:00 | 7:00 | 8:00 | 9:00 | 10:00 | 11:00 | 12:00 PM | 1:00 | 2:00 | 3:00 | 4:00 | 5:00 | 6:00 |

TO DO LIST

MY MOODS

FOR TOMORROW

QUICK NOTE

TO DO LIST

HEALTH & FITNESS

WATER INTAKE

TODAY'S NOTES

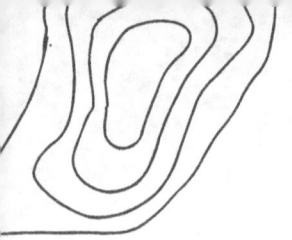

GOOD MORNING!!

___/___/___

M T W T F S S
○ ○ ○ ○ ○ ○ ○

TODAY'S APPOINTMENTS

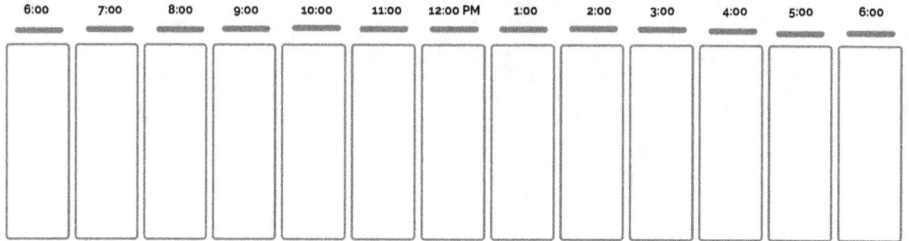

6:00	7:00	8:00	9:00	10:00	11:00	12:00 PM	1:00	2:00	3:00	4:00	5:00	6:00

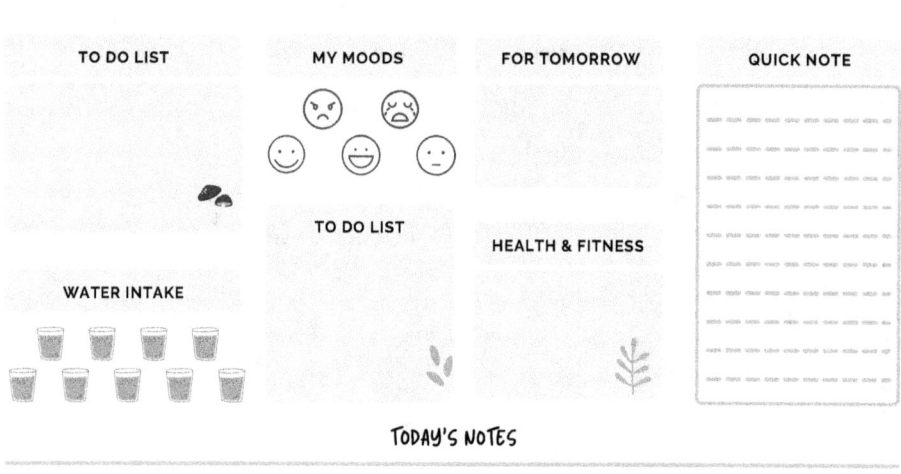

TO DO LIST

MY MOODS

FOR TOMORROW

QUICK NOTE

TO DO LIST

WATER INTAKE

HEALTH & FITNESS

TODAY'S NOTES

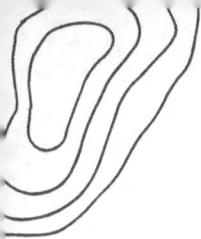

GOOD MORNING!!

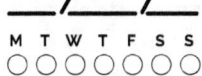

M T W T F S S
◯ ◯ ◯ ◯ ◯ ◯ ◯

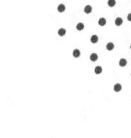

TODAY'S APPOINTMENTS

6:00	7:00	8:00	9:00	10:00	11:00	12:00 PM	1:00	2:00	3:00	4:00	5:00	6:00

TO DO LIST

MY MOODS

FOR TOMORROW

QUICK NOTE

WATER INTAKE

TO DO LIST

HEALTH & FITNESS

TODAY'S NOTES

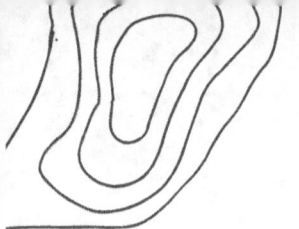

GOOD MORNING!!

___/___/___

M T W T F S S
○ ○ ○ ○ ○ ○ ○

TODAY'S APPOINTMENTS

6:00	7:00	8:00	9:00	10:00	11:00	12:00 PM	1:00	2:00	3:00	4:00	5:00	6:00

TO DO LIST

MY MOODS

FOR TOMORROW

QUICK NOTE

TO DO LIST

WATER INTAKE

HEALTH & FITNESS

TODAY'S NOTES

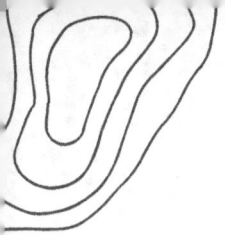
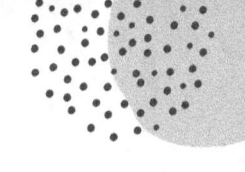

GOOD MORNING!!

___ / ___ / ___

M T W T F S S
○ ○ ○ ○ ○ ○ ○

TODAY'S APPOINTMENTS

6:00	7:00	8:00	9:00	10:00	11:00	12:00 PM	1:00	2:00	3:00	4:00	5:00	6:00

TO DO LIST

MY MOODS

FOR TOMORROW

QUICK NOTE

TO DO LIST

HEALTH & FITNESS

WATER INTAKE

TODAY'S NOTES

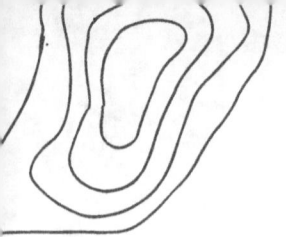

GOOD MORNING!!

___/___/___

M T W T F S S
○ ○ ○ ○ ○ ○ ○

TODAY'S APPOINTMENTS

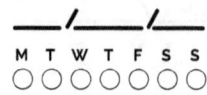

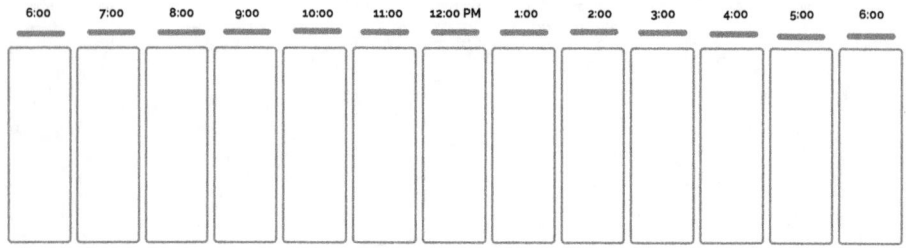

6:00	7:00	8:00	9:00	10:00	11:00	12:00 PM	1:00	2:00	3:00	4:00	5:00	6:00

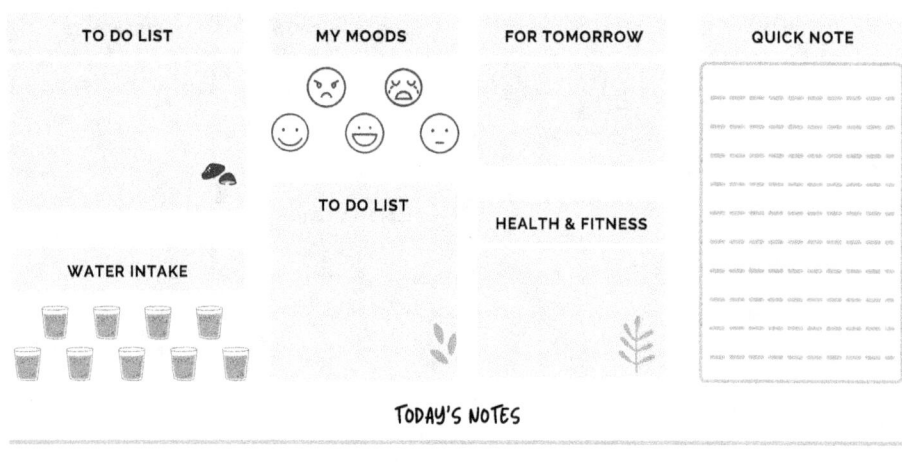

TO DO LIST	MY MOODS	FOR TOMORROW	QUICK NOTE

TO DO LIST

HEALTH & FITNESS

WATER INTAKE

TODAY'S NOTES

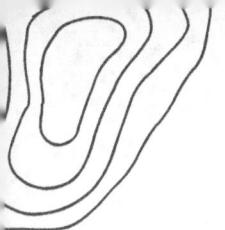

GOOD MORNING!!

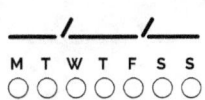

M T W T F S S
○ ○ ○ ○ ○ ○ ○

TODAY'S APPOINTMENTS

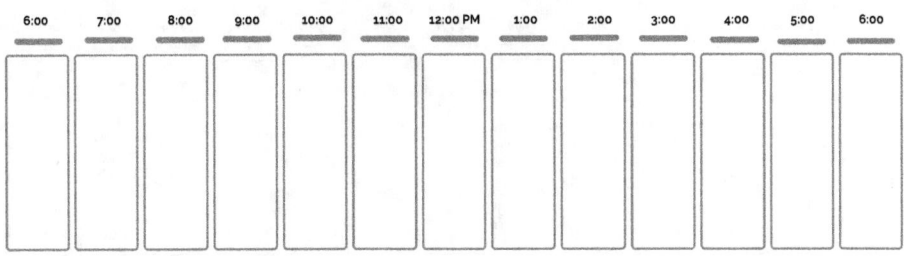

6:00	7:00	8:00	9:00	10:00	11:00	12:00 PM	1:00	2:00	3:00	4:00	5:00	6:00

TO DO LIST

MY MOODS

FOR TOMORROW

QUICK NOTE

TO DO LIST

WATER INTAKE

HEALTH & FITNESS

TODAY'S NOTES

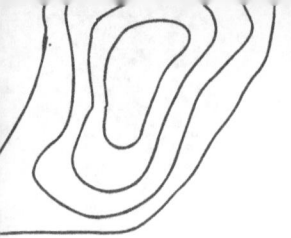

GOOD MORNING!!

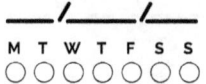

M T W T F S S
◯ ◯ ◯ ◯ ◯ ◯ ◯

TODAY'S APPOINTMENTS

6:00	7:00	8:00	9:00	10:00	11:00	12:00 PM	1:00	2:00	3:00	4:00	5:00	6:00

TO DO LIST

MY MOODS

FOR TOMORROW

QUICK NOTE

TO DO LIST

HEALTH & FITNESS

WATER INTAKE

TODAY'S NOTES

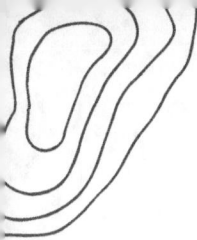

GOOD MORNING!!

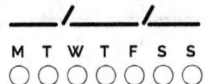

M T W T F S S
○ ○ ○ ○ ○ ○ ○

TODAY'S APPOINTMENTS

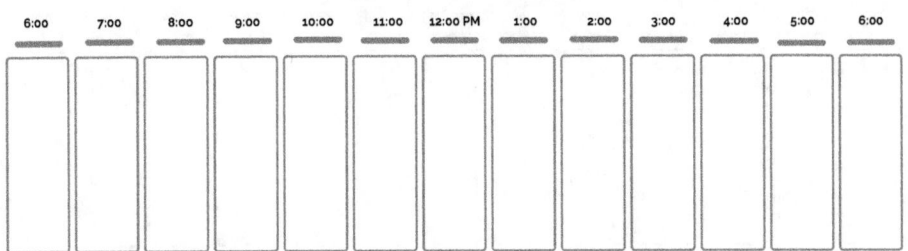

6:00	7:00	8:00	9:00	10:00	11:00	12:00 PM	1:00	2:00	3:00	4:00	5:00	6:00

TO DO LIST

MY MOODS

FOR TOMORROW

QUICK NOTE

TO DO LIST

HEALTH & FITNESS

WATER INTAKE

TODAY'S NOTES

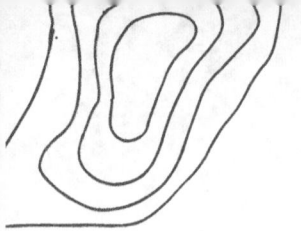

GOOD MORNING!!

___/___/___

M T W T F S S
○ ○ ○ ○ ○ ○ ○

TODAY'S APPOINTMENTS

6:00	7:00	8:00	9:00	10:00	11:00	12:00 PM	1:00	2:00	3:00	4:00	5:00	6:00

TO DO LIST

MY MOODS

FOR TOMORROW

QUICK NOTE

TO DO LIST

WATER INTAKE

HEALTH & FITNESS

TODAY'S NOTES

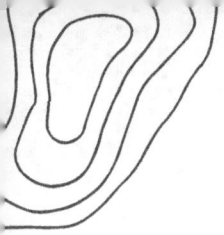

GOOD MORNING!!

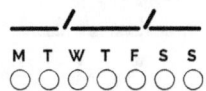

M T W T F S S
○ ○ ○ ○ ○ ○ ○

TODAY'S APPOINTMENTS

6:00	7:00	8:00	9:00	10:00	11:00	12:00 PM	1:00	2:00	3:00	4:00	5:00	6:00

TO DO LIST

MY MOODS

FOR TOMORROW

QUICK NOTE

TO DO LIST

WATER INTAKE

HEALTH & FITNESS

TODAY'S NOTES

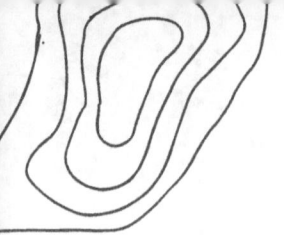

GooD MorNInG!!

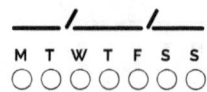

M T W T F S S
○ ○ ○ ○ ○ ○ ○

TODAY'S APPOINTMENTS

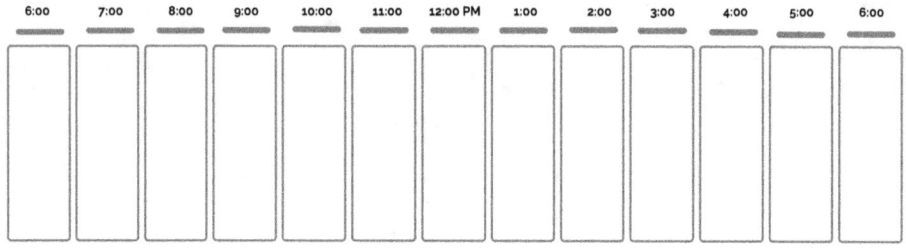

6:00	7:00	8:00	9:00	10:00	11:00	12:00 PM	1:00	2:00	3:00	4:00	5:00	6:00

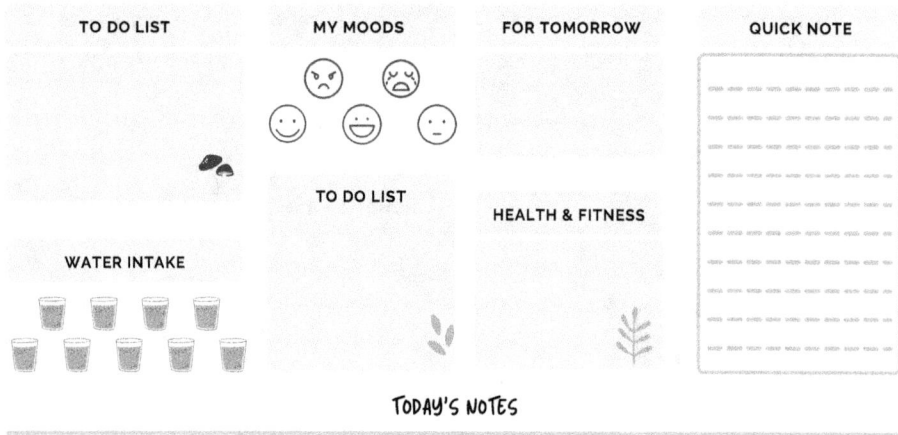

TO DO LIST

MY MOODS

FOR TOMORROW

QUICK NOTE

TO DO LIST

HEALTH & FITNESS

WATER INTAKE

TODAY'S NOTES

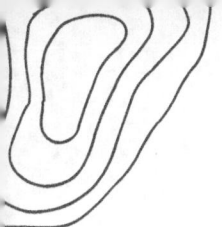

GOOD MORNING!!

___/___/___

M T W T F S S
○ ○ ○ ○ ○ ○ ○

TODAY'S APPOINTMENTS

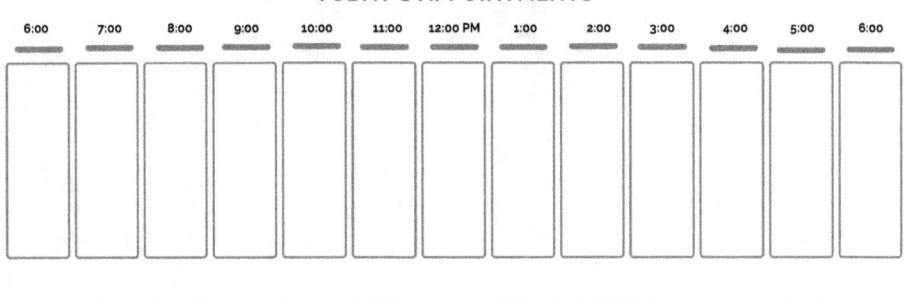

| 6:00 | 7:00 | 8:00 | 9:00 | 10:00 | 11:00 | 12:00 PM | 1:00 | 2:00 | 3:00 | 4:00 | 5:00 | 6:00 |

TO DO LIST

MY MOODS

FOR TOMORROW

QUICK NOTE

TO DO LIST

HEALTH & FITNESS

WATER INTAKE

TODAY'S NOTES

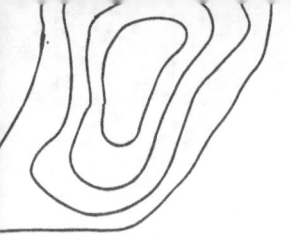

GooD MorNiNG!!

___/___/___

M T W T F S S
○ ○ ○ ○ ○ ○ ○

TODAY'S APPOINTMENTS

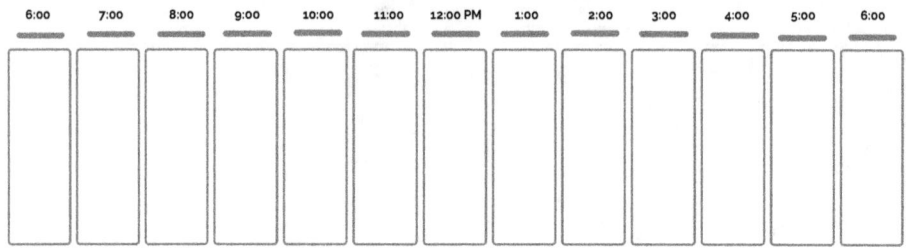

6:00	7:00	8:00	9:00	10:00	11:00	12:00 PM	1:00	2:00	3:00	4:00	5:00	6:00

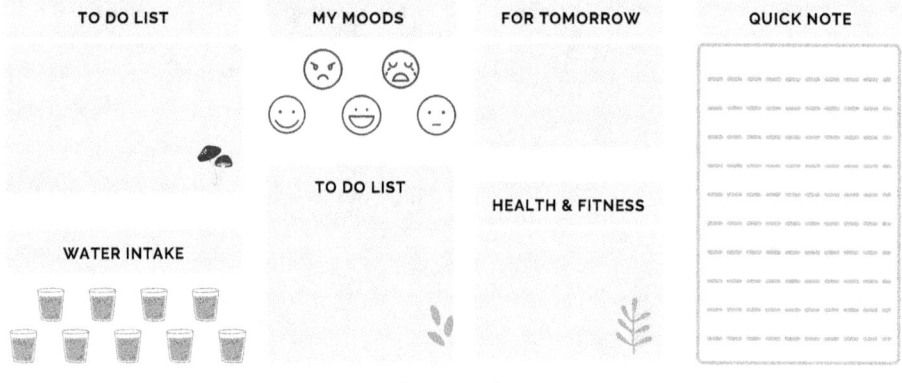

TO DO LIST

MY MOODS

FOR TOMORROW

QUICK NOTE

WATER INTAKE

TO DO LIST

HEALTH & FITNESS

TODAY'S NOTES

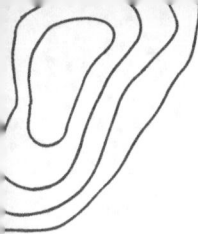

GOOD MORNING!!

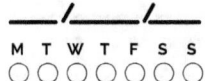

M T W T F S S
○ ○ ○ ○ ○ ○ ○

TODAY'S APPOINTMENTS

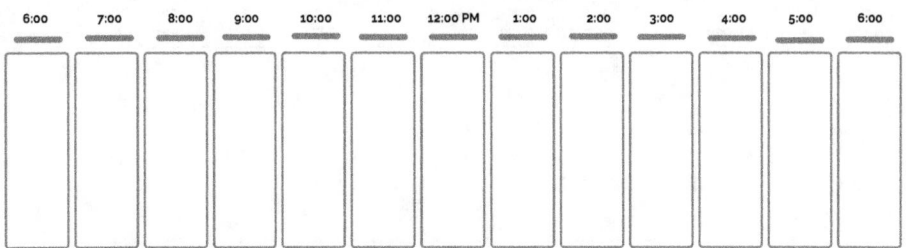

6:00	7:00	8:00	9:00	10:00	11:00	12:00 PM	1:00	2:00	3:00	4:00	5:00	6:00

TO DO LIST

MY MOODS

FOR TOMORROW

QUICK NOTE

WATER INTAKE

TO DO LIST

HEALTH & FITNESS

TODAY'S NOTES

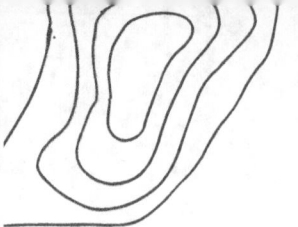

GooD MoRNING!!

___/___/___

M T W T F S S
○ ○ ○ ○ ○ ○ ○

TODAY'S APPOINTMENTS

6:00	7:00	8:00	9:00	10:00	11:00	12:00 PM	1:00	2:00	3:00	4:00	5:00	6:00

TO DO LIST

MY MOODS

FOR TOMORROW

QUICK NOTE

TO DO LIST

WATER INTAKE

HEALTH & FITNESS

TODAY'S NOTES

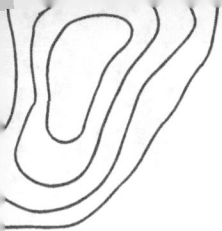

GOOD MORNING!!

___/___/___

M T W T F S S
◯ ◯ ◯ ◯ ◯ ◯ ◯

TODAY'S APPOINTMENTS

6:00	7:00	8:00	9:00	10:00	11:00	12:00 PM	1:00	2:00	3:00	4:00	5:00	6:00

TO DO LIST

MY MOODS

FOR TOMORROW

QUICK NOTE

TO DO LIST

HEALTH & FITNESS

WATER INTAKE

TODAY'S NOTES

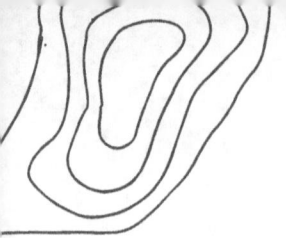

GOOD MORNING!!

___ / ___ / ___

M T W T F S S
○ ○ ○ ○ ○ ○ ○

TODAY'S APPOINTMENTS

6:00	7:00	8:00	9:00	10:00	11:00	12:00 PM	1:00	2:00	3:00	4:00	5:00	6:00

TO DO LIST

MY MOODS

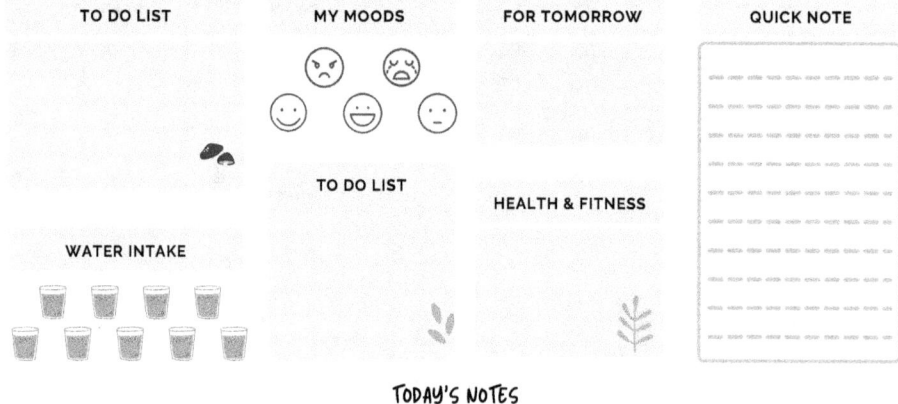

FOR TOMORROW

QUICK NOTE

TO DO LIST

HEALTH & FITNESS

WATER INTAKE

TODAY'S NOTES

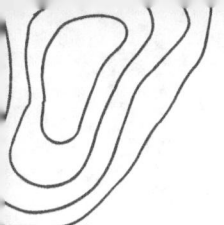

GOOD MORNING!!

___/___/___

M T W T F S S
○ ○ ○ ○ ○ ○ ○

TODAY'S APPOINTMENTS

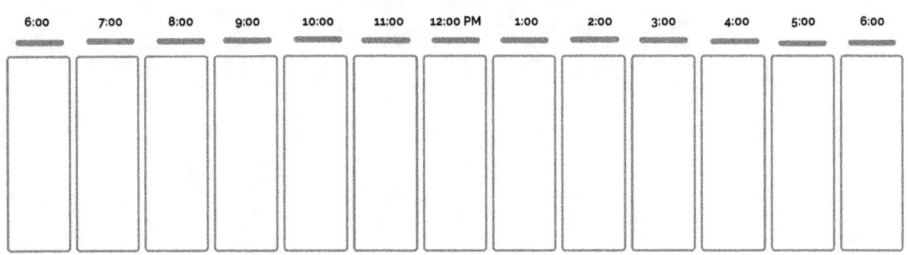

| 6:00 | 7:00 | 8:00 | 9:00 | 10:00 | 11:00 | 12:00 PM | 1:00 | 2:00 | 3:00 | 4:00 | 5:00 | 6:00 |

TO DO LIST

MY MOODS

FOR TOMORROW

QUICK NOTE

TO DO LIST

HEALTH & FITNESS

WATER INTAKE

TODAY'S NOTES

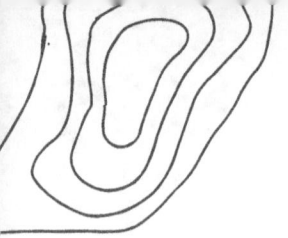

GOOD MORNING!!

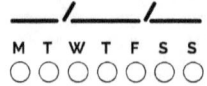

M T W T F S S
○ ○ ○ ○ ○ ○ ○

TODAY'S APPOINTMENTS

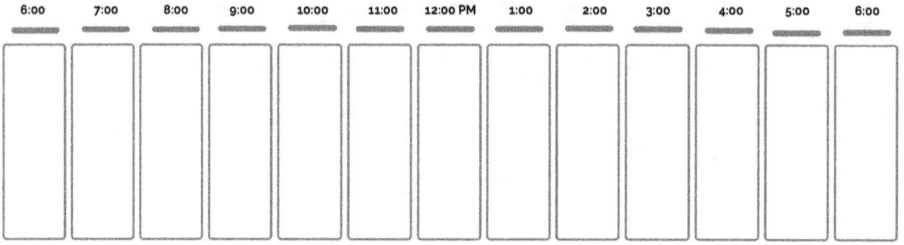

6:00	7:00	8:00	9:00	10:00	11:00	12:00 PM	1:00	2:00	3:00	4:00	5:00	6:00

TO DO LIST

MY MOODS

FOR TOMORROW

QUICK NOTE

TO DO LIST

HEALTH & FITNESS

WATER INTAKE

TODAY'S NOTES

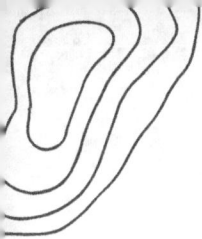
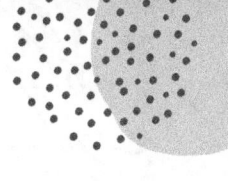

GOOD MORNING!!

___/___/___

M T W T F S S
○ ○ ○ ○ ○ ○ ○

TODAY'S APPOINTMENTS

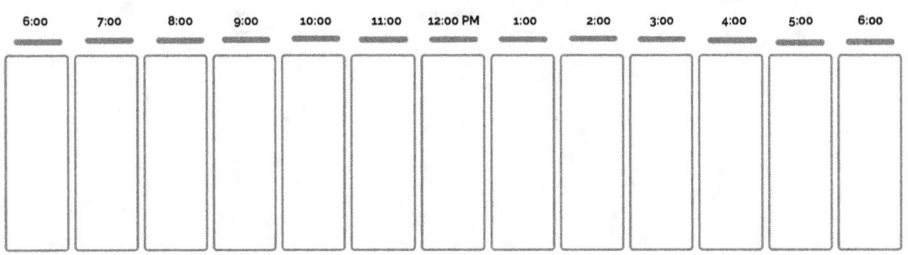

6:00	7:00	8:00	9:00	10:00	11:00	12:00 PM	1:00	2:00	3:00	4:00	5:00	6:00

TO DO LIST

MY MOODS

FOR TOMORROW

QUICK NOTE

TO DO LIST

HEALTH & FITNESS

WATER INTAKE

TODAY'S NOTES

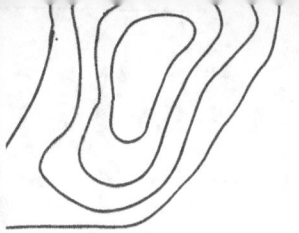

GOOD MORNING!!

___/___/___

M T W T F S S
○ ○ ○ ○ ○ ○ ○

TODAY'S APPOINTMENTS

6:00	7:00	8:00	9:00	10:00	11:00	12:00 PM	1:00	2:00	3:00	4:00	5:00	6:00

TO DO LIST

MY MOODS

FOR TOMORROW

QUICK NOTE

TO DO LIST

HEALTH & FITNESS

WATER INTAKE

TODAY'S NOTES

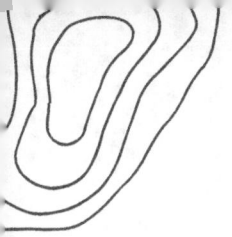

GOOD MORNING!!

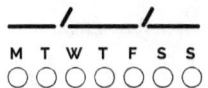

M T W T F S S
○ ○ ○ ○ ○ ○ ○

TODAY'S APPOINTMENTS

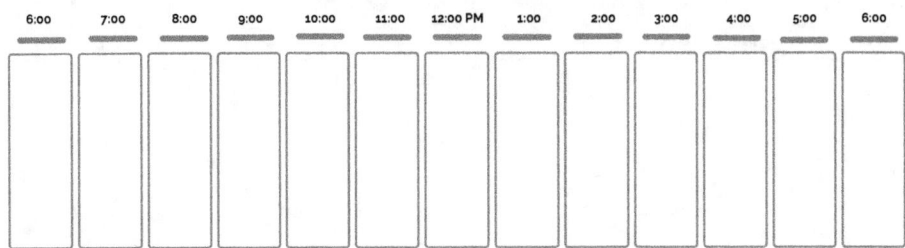

6:00	7:00	8:00	9:00	10:00	11:00	12:00 PM	1:00	2:00	3:00	4:00	5:00	6:00

TO DO LIST

MY MOODS

FOR TOMORROW

QUICK NOTE

TO DO LIST

HEALTH & FITNESS

WATER INTAKE

TODAY'S NOTES

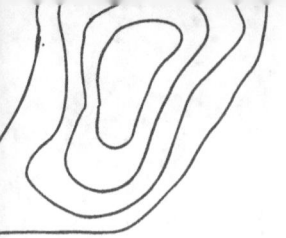

GOOD MORNING!!

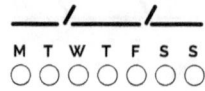

M T W T F S S
○ ○ ○ ○ ○ ○ ○

TODAY'S APPOINTMENTS

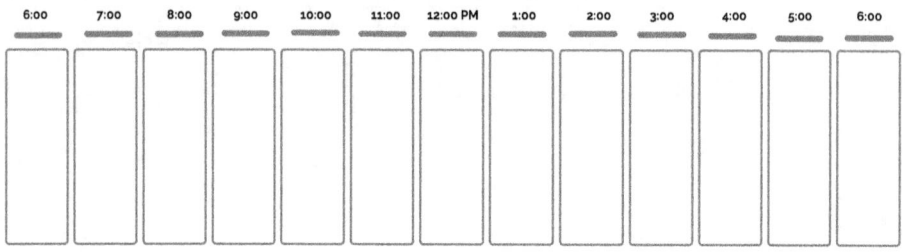

6:00	7:00	8:00	9:00	10:00	11:00	12:00 PM	1:00	2:00	3:00	4:00	5:00	6:00

TO DO LIST

MY MOODS

FOR TOMORROW

QUICK NOTE

TO DO LIST

HEALTH & FITNESS

WATER INTAKE

TODAY'S NOTES

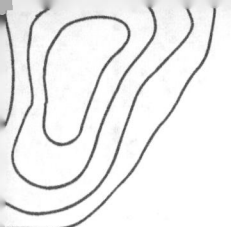

GOOD MORNING!!

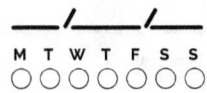

M T W T F S S
○ ○ ○ ○ ○ ○ ○

TODAY'S APPOINTMENTS

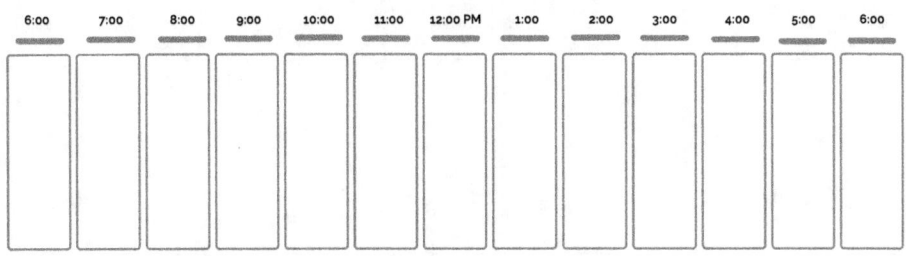

6:00	7:00	8:00	9:00	10:00	11:00	12:00 PM	1:00	2:00	3:00	4:00	5:00	6:00

TO DO LIST

MY MOODS

FOR TOMORROW

QUICK NOTE

TO DO LIST

WATER INTAKE

HEALTH & FITNESS

TODAY'S NOTES

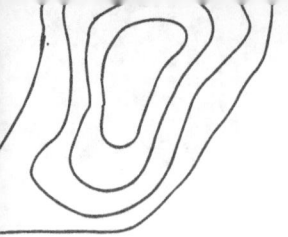

GOOD MORNING!!

___/___/___

M T W T F S S
◯ ◯ ◯ ◯ ◯ ◯ ◯

TODAY'S APPOINTMENTS

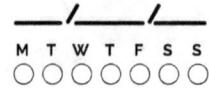

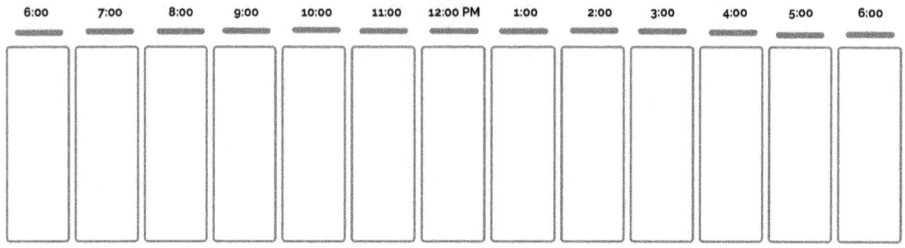

6:00	7:00	8:00	9:00	10:00	11:00	12:00 PM	1:00	2:00	3:00	4:00	5:00	6:00

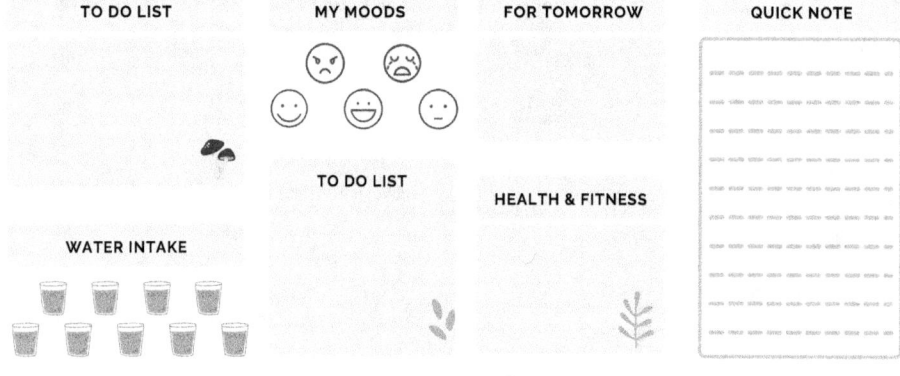

TO DO LIST

MY MOODS

FOR TOMORROW

QUICK NOTE

TO DO LIST

HEALTH & FITNESS

WATER INTAKE

TODAY'S NOTES

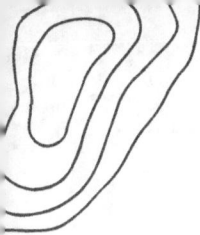
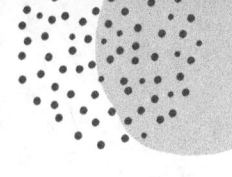

GooD MorNiNG!!

___ / ___ / ___

M T W T F S S
○ ○ ○ ○ ○ ○ ○

TODAY'S APPOINTMENTS

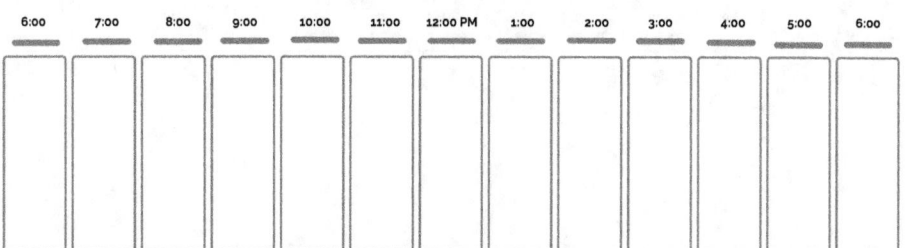

6:00	7:00	8:00	9:00	10:00	11:00	12:00 PM	1:00	2:00	3:00	4:00	5:00	6:00

TO DO LIST

MY MOODS

FOR TOMORROW

QUICK NOTE

TO DO LIST

HEALTH & FITNESS

WATER INTAKE

TODAY'S NOTES

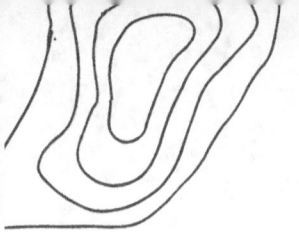

GooD MoRNING!!

____/____/____

M T W T F S S
○ ○ ○ ○ ○ ○ ○

TODAY'S APPOINTMENTS

6:00	7:00	8:00	9:00	10:00	11:00	12:00 PM	1:00	2:00	3:00	4:00	5:00	6:00

TO DO LIST

MY MOODS

FOR TOMORROW

QUICK NOTE

TO DO LIST

WATER INTAKE

HEALTH & FITNESS

TODAY'S NOTES

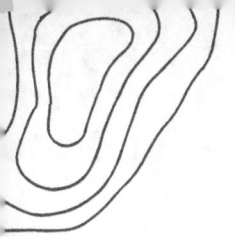
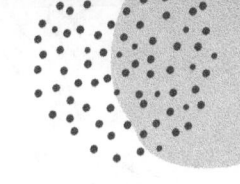

GOOD MORNING!!

___/___/___

M T W T F S S
○ ○ ○ ○ ○ ○ ○

TODAY'S APPOINTMENTS

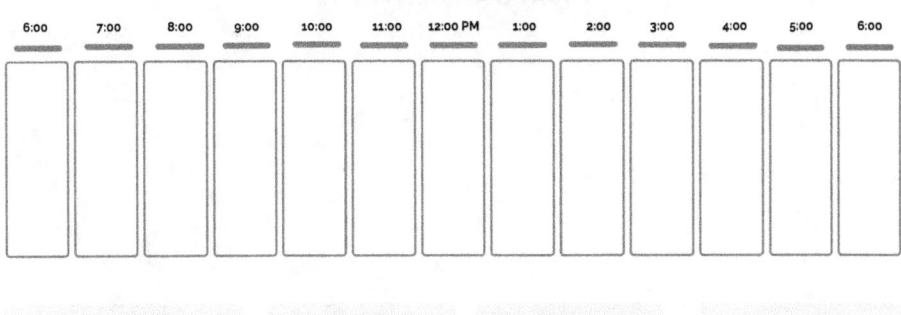

6:00	7:00	8:00	9:00	10:00	11:00	12:00 PM	1:00	2:00	3:00	4:00	5:00	6:00

TO DO LIST

MY MOODS

FOR TOMORROW

QUICK NOTE

TO DO LIST

HEALTH & FITNESS

WATER INTAKE

TODAY'S NOTES

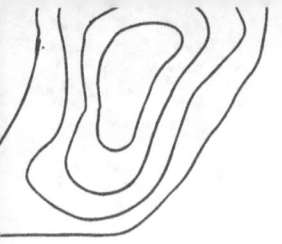

GOOD MORNING!!

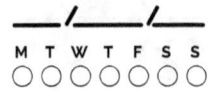

M T W T F S S
○ ○ ○ ○ ○ ○ ○

TODAY'S APPOINTMENTS

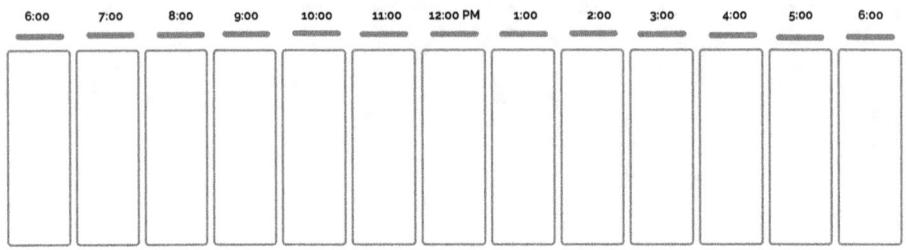

6:00	7:00	8:00	9:00	10:00	11:00	12:00 PM	1:00	2:00	3:00	4:00	5:00	6:00

TO DO LIST

MY MOODS

FOR TOMORROW

QUICK NOTE

TO DO LIST

HEALTH & FITNESS

WATER INTAKE

TODAY'S NOTES

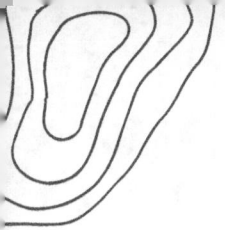

GOOD MORNING!!

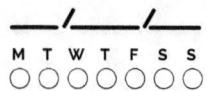

M T W T F S S
○ ○ ○ ○ ○ ○ ○

TODAY'S APPOINTMENTS

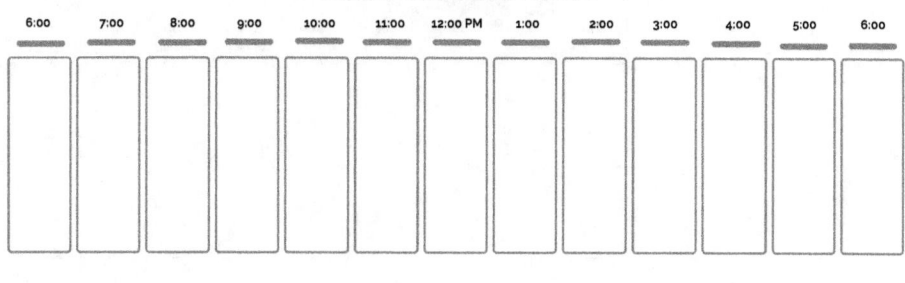

6:00	7:00	8:00	9:00	10:00	11:00	12:00 PM	1:00	2:00	3:00	4:00	5:00	6:00

TO DO LIST

MY MOODS

FOR TOMORROW

QUICK NOTE

TO DO LIST

HEALTH & FITNESS

WATER INTAKE

TODAY'S NOTES

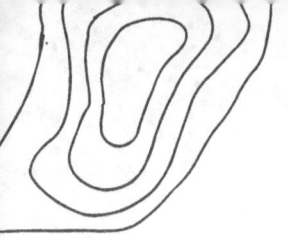

GOOD MORNING!!

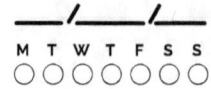

M T W T F S S
○ ○ ○ ○ ○ ○ ○

TODAY'S APPOINTMENTS

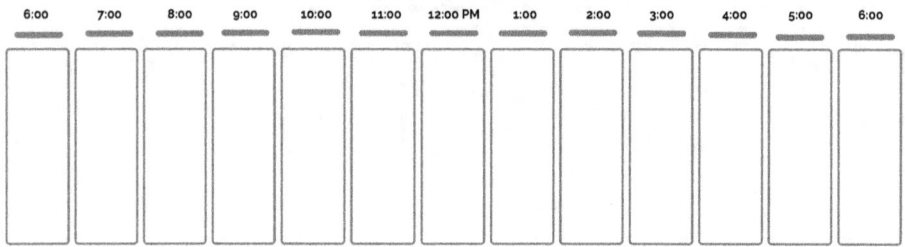

6:00	7:00	8:00	9:00	10:00	11:00	12:00 PM	1:00	2:00	3:00	4:00	5:00	6:00

TO DO LIST

MY MOODS

FOR TOMORROW

QUICK NOTE

TO DO LIST

HEALTH & FITNESS

WATER INTAKE

TODAY'S NOTES

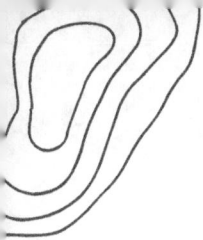
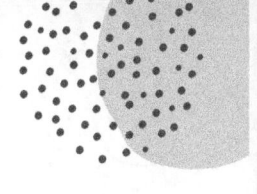

GOOD MORNING!!

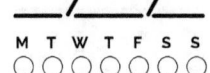

M T W T F S S
○ ○ ○ ○ ○ ○ ○

TODAY'S APPOINTMENTS

6:00	7:00	8:00	9:00	10:00	11:00	12:00 PM	1:00	2:00	3:00	4:00	5:00	6:00

TO DO LIST

MY MOODS

FOR TOMORROW

QUICK NOTE

WATER INTAKE

TO DO LIST

HEALTH & FITNESS

TODAY'S NOTES

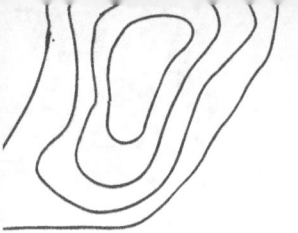

GOOD MORNING!!

___/___/___

M T W T F S S
○ ○ ○ ○ ○ ○ ○

TODAY'S APPOINTMENTS

6:00	7:00	8:00	9:00	10:00	11:00	12:00 PM	1:00	2:00	3:00	4:00	5:00	6:00

TO DO LIST

MY MOODS

FOR TOMORROW

QUICK NOTE

TO DO LIST

HEALTH & FITNESS

WATER INTAKE

TODAY'S NOTES

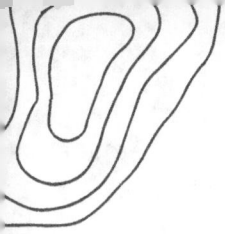

GOOD MORNING!!

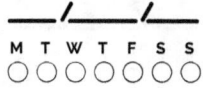

___ / ___ / ___

M T W T F S S
○ ○ ○ ○ ○ ○ ○

TODAY'S APPOINTMENTS

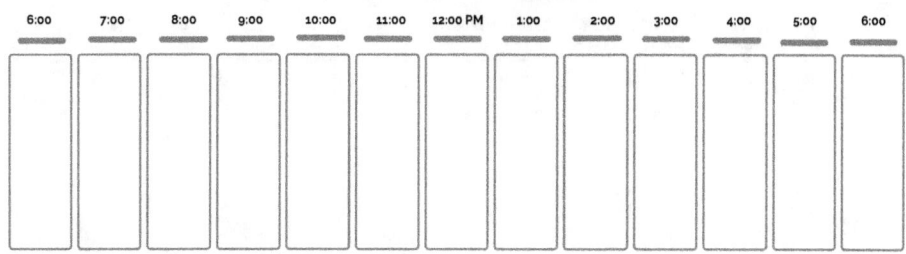

6:00	7:00	8:00	9:00	10:00	11:00	12:00 PM	1:00	2:00	3:00	4:00	5:00	6:00

TO DO LIST

MY MOODS

FOR TOMORROW

QUICK NOTE

TO DO LIST

HEALTH & FITNESS

WATER INTAKE

TODAY'S NOTES

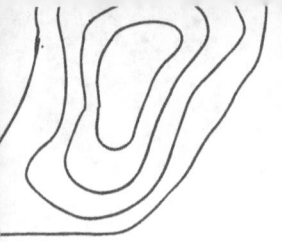

GOOD MORNING!!

___ / ___ / ___

M T W T F S S
○ ○ ○ ○ ○ ○ ○

TODAY'S APPOINTMENTS

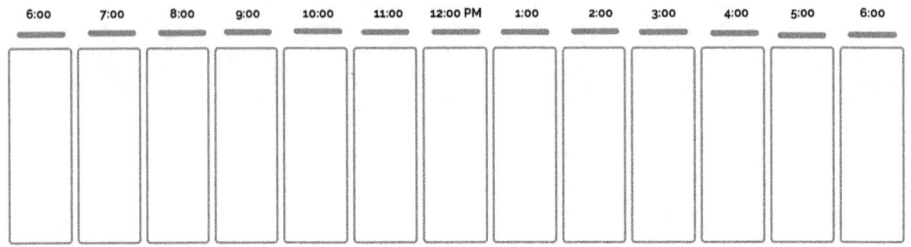

6:00	7:00	8:00	9:00	10:00	11:00	12:00 PM	1:00	2:00	3:00	4:00	5:00	6:00

TO DO LIST

MY MOODS

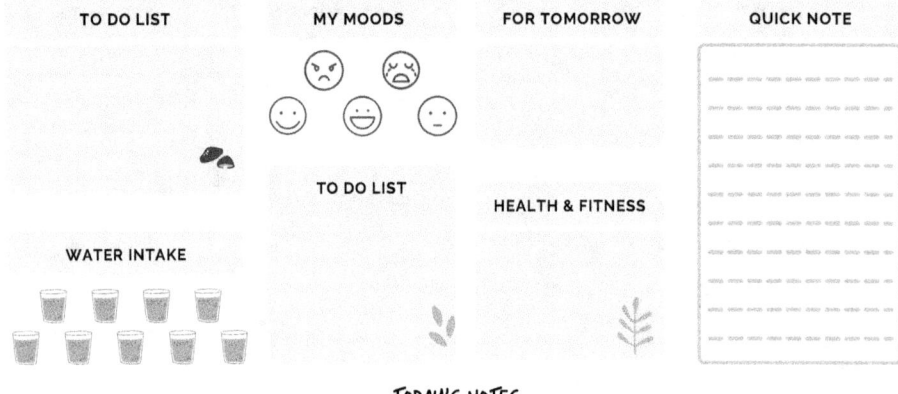

FOR TOMORROW

QUICK NOTE

TO DO LIST

WATER INTAKE

HEALTH & FITNESS

TODAY'S NOTES

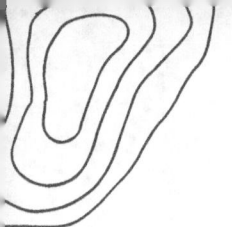

GooD MorNING!!

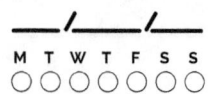

M T W T F S S
○ ○ ○ ○ ○ ○ ○

TODAY'S APPOINTMENTS

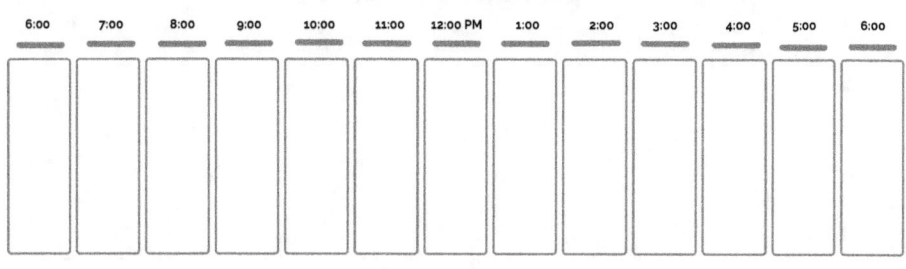

6:00	7:00	8:00	9:00	10:00	11:00	12:00 PM	1:00	2:00	3:00	4:00	5:00	6:00

TO DO LIST

MY MOODS

FOR TOMORROW

QUICK NOTE

TO DO LIST

HEALTH & FITNESS

WATER INTAKE

TODAY'S NOTES

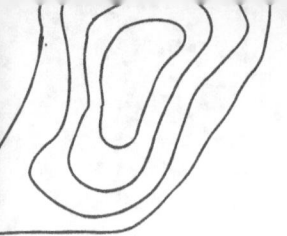

GOOD MORNING!!

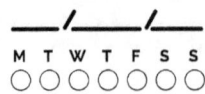

M T W T F S S
○ ○ ○ ○ ○ ○ ○

TODAY'S APPOINTMENTS

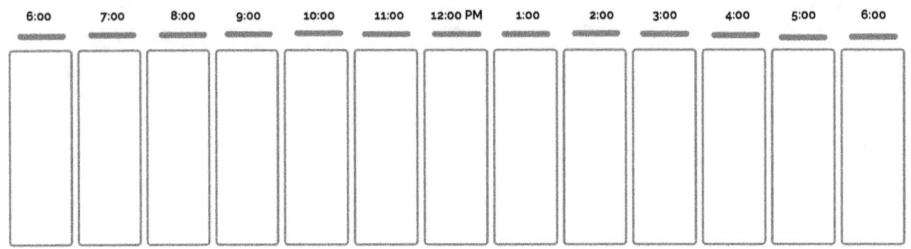

6:00	7:00	8:00	9:00	10:00	11:00	12:00 PM	1:00	2:00	3:00	4:00	5:00	6:00

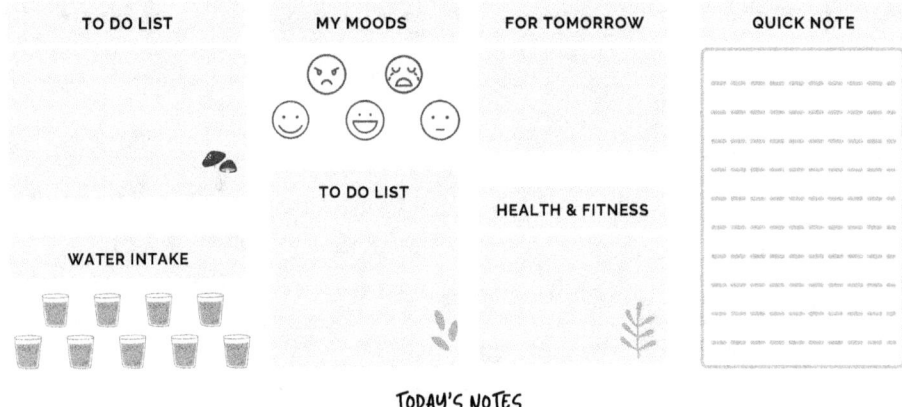

TO DO LIST

MY MOODS

FOR TOMORROW

QUICK NOTE

WATER INTAKE

TO DO LIST

HEALTH & FITNESS

TODAY'S NOTES

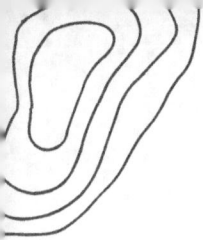
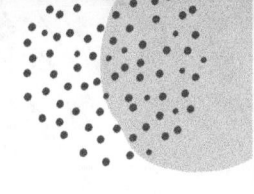

GOOD MORNING!!

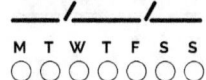

M T W T F S S
○ ○ ○ ○ ○ ○ ○

TODAY'S APPOINTMENTS

6:00	7:00	8:00	9:00	10:00	11:00	12:00 PM	1:00	2:00	3:00	4:00	5:00	6:00

TO DO LIST

MY MOODS

FOR TOMORROW

QUICK NOTE

WATER INTAKE

TO DO LIST

HEALTH & FITNESS

TODAY'S NOTES

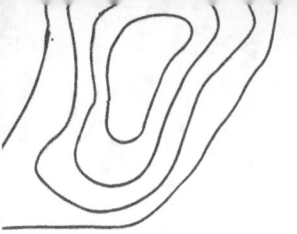

GOOD MORNING!!

___/___/___

M T W T F S S
○ ○ ○ ○ ○ ○ ○

TODAY'S APPOINTMENTS

6:00	7:00	8:00	9:00	10:00	11:00	12:00 PM	1:00	2:00	3:00	4:00	5:00	6:00

TO DO LIST

MY MOODS

FOR TOMORROW

QUICK NOTE

TO DO LIST

WATER INTAKE

HEALTH & FITNESS

TODAY'S NOTES

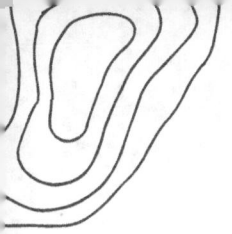

GOOD MORNING!!

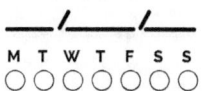

M T W T F S S
○ ○ ○ ○ ○ ○ ○

TODAY'S APPOINTMENTS

6:00	7:00	8:00	9:00	10:00	11:00	12:00 PM	1:00	2:00	3:00	4:00	5:00	6:00

TO DO LIST

MY MOODS

FOR TOMORROW

QUICK NOTE

TO DO LIST

WATER INTAKE

HEALTH & FITNESS

TODAY'S NOTES

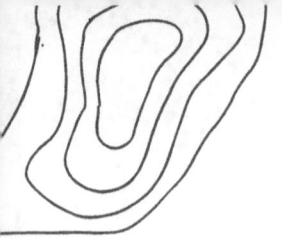

GOOD MORNING!!

___/___/___

M T W T F S S
○ ○ ○ ○ ○ ○ ○

TODAY'S APPOINTMENTS

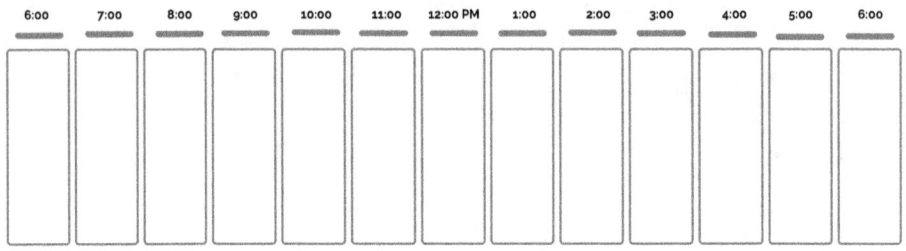

6:00	7:00	8:00	9:00	10:00	11:00	12:00 PM	1:00	2:00	3:00	4:00	5:00	6:00

TO DO LIST

MY MOODS

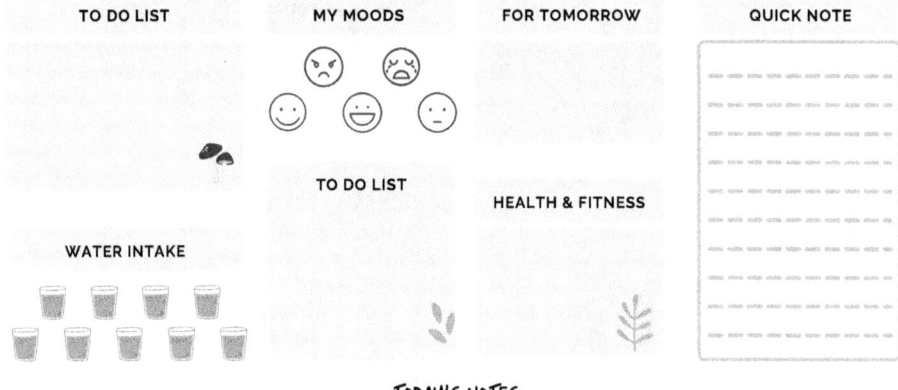

FOR TOMORROW

QUICK NOTE

TO DO LIST

HEALTH & FITNESS

WATER INTAKE

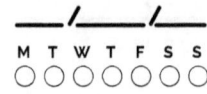

TODAY'S NOTES

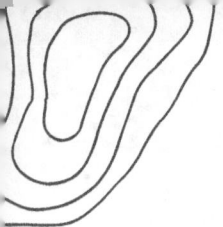

GOOD MORNING!!

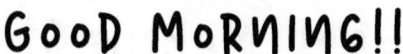

M T W T F S S
◯ ◯ ◯ ◯ ◯ ◯ ◯

TODAY'S APPOINTMENTS

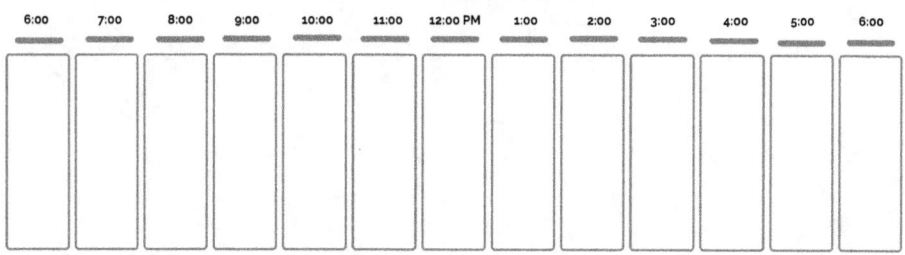

| 6:00 | 7:00 | 8:00 | 9:00 | 10:00 | 11:00 | 12:00 PM | 1:00 | 2:00 | 3:00 | 4:00 | 5:00 | 6:00 |

TO DO LIST

MY MOODS

FOR TOMORROW

QUICK NOTE

TO DO LIST

HEALTH & FITNESS

WATER INTAKE

TODAY'S NOTES

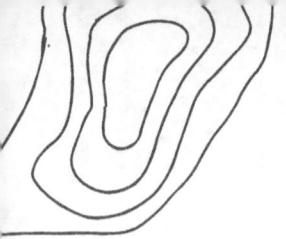

GOOD MORNING!!

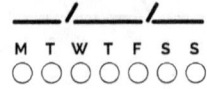

M T W T F S S
○ ○ ○ ○ ○ ○ ○

TODAY'S APPOINTMENTS

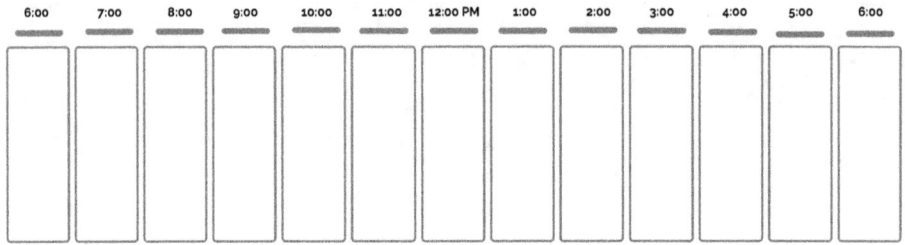

6:00	7:00	8:00	9:00	10:00	11:00	12:00 PM	1:00	2:00	3:00	4:00	5:00	6:00

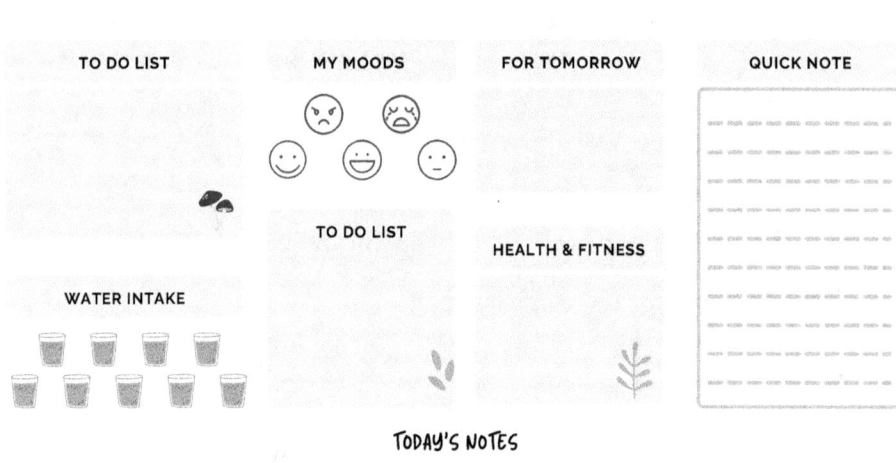

TO DO LIST

MY MOODS

FOR TOMORROW

QUICK NOTE

TO DO LIST

WATER INTAKE

HEALTH & FITNESS

TODAY'S NOTES

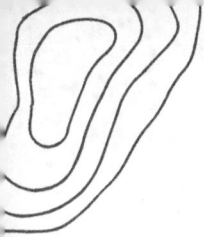
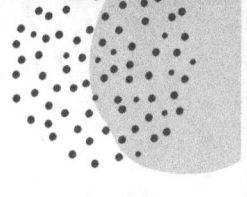

GooD MorNING!!

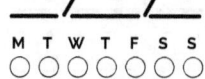

M T W T F S S
○ ○ ○ ○ ○ ○ ○

TODAY'S APPOINTMENTS

6:00	7:00	8:00	9:00	10:00	11:00	12:00 PM	1:00	2:00	3:00	4:00	5:00	6:00

TO DO LIST

MY MOODS

FOR TOMORROW

QUICK NOTE

WATER INTAKE

TO DO LIST

HEALTH & FITNESS

TODAY'S NOTES

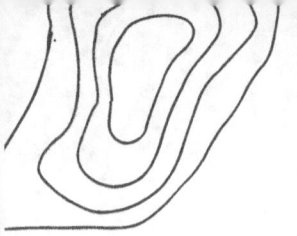

GOOD MORNING!!

___/___/___

M T W T F S S
○ ○ ○ ○ ○ ○ ○

TODAY'S APPOINTMENTS

6:00	7:00	8:00	9:00	10:00	11:00	12:00 PM	1:00	2:00	3:00	4:00	5:00	6:00

TO DO LIST

MY MOODS

FOR TOMORROW

QUICK NOTE

TO DO LIST

HEALTH & FITNESS

WATER INTAKE

TODAY'S NOTES

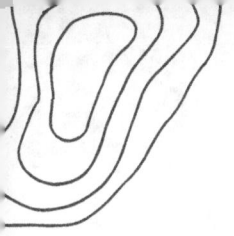

GOOD MORNING!!

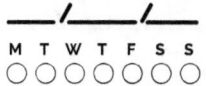

M T W T F S S
○ ○ ○ ○ ○ ○ ○

TODAY'S APPOINTMENTS

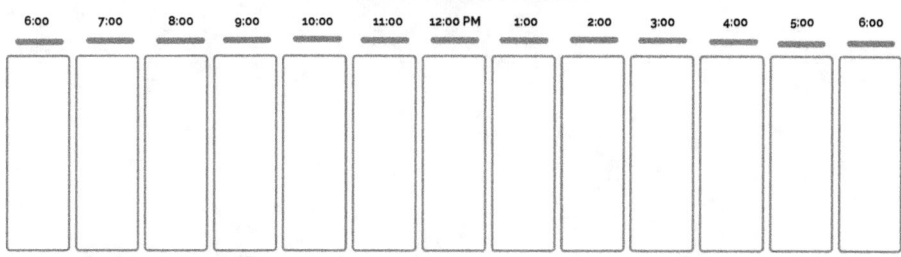

6:00	7:00	8:00	9:00	10:00	11:00	12:00 PM	1:00	2:00	3:00	4:00	5:00	6:00

TO DO LIST

MY MOODS

FOR TOMORROW

QUICK NOTE

TO DO LIST

HEALTH & FITNESS

WATER INTAKE

TODAY'S NOTES

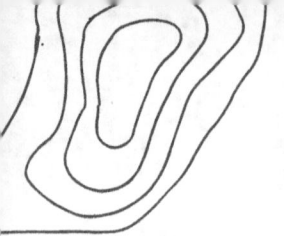

GooD MorNINg!!

___/___/___

M T W T F S S
○ ○ ○ ○ ○ ○ ○

TODAY'S APPOINTMENTS

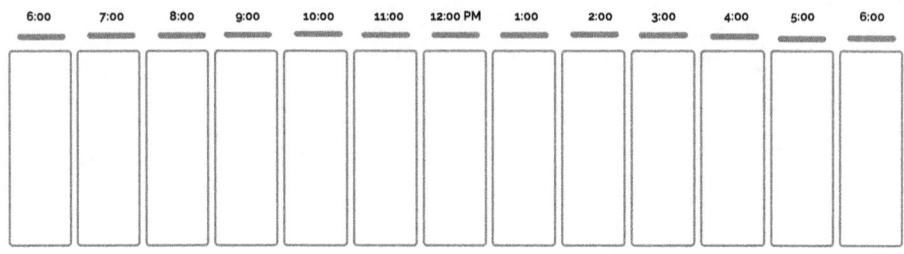

6:00	7:00	8:00	9:00	10:00	11:00	12:00 PM	1:00	2:00	3:00	4:00	5:00	6:00

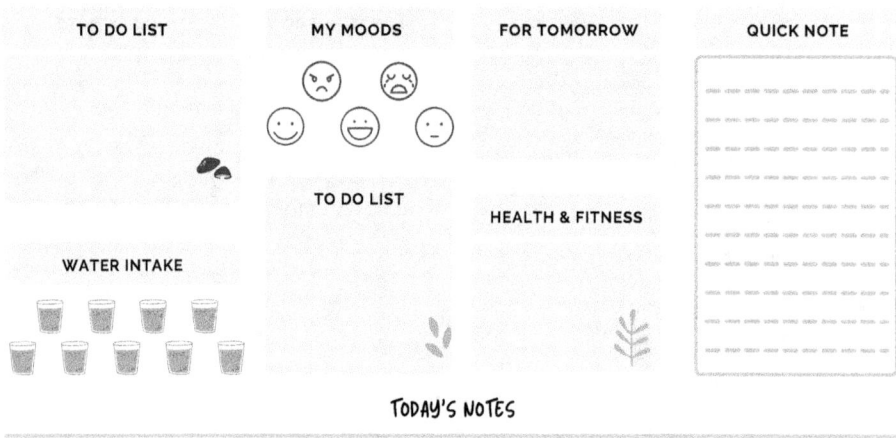

TO DO LIST

MY MOODS

FOR TOMORROW

QUICK NOTE

TO DO LIST

HEALTH & FITNESS

WATER INTAKE

TODAY'S NOTES

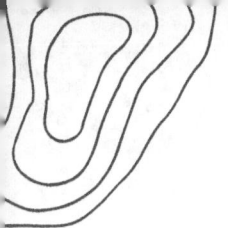

GOOD MORNING!!

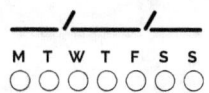

___/___/___

M T W T F S S
○ ○ ○ ○ ○ ○ ○

TODAY'S APPOINTMENTS

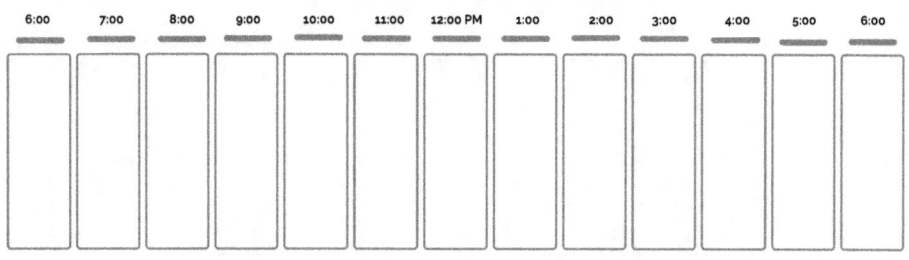

6:00	7:00	8:00	9:00	10:00	11:00	12:00 PM	1:00	2:00	3:00	4:00	5:00	6:00

TO DO LIST

MY MOODS

FOR TOMORROW

QUICK NOTE

TO DO LIST

HEALTH & FITNESS

WATER INTAKE

TODAY'S NOTES

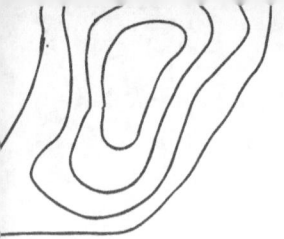

GOOD MORNING!!

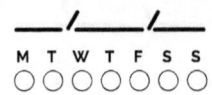

M T W T F S S
○ ○ ○ ○ ○ ○ ○

TODAY'S APPOINTMENTS

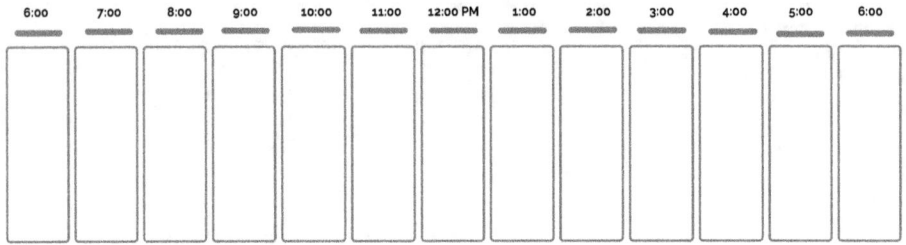

6:00	7:00	8:00	9:00	10:00	11:00	12:00 PM	1:00	2:00	3:00	4:00	5:00	6:00

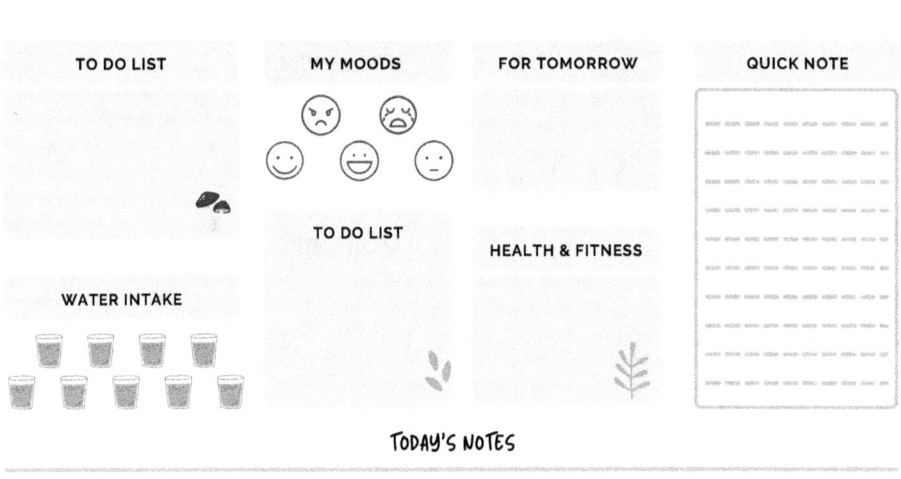

TO DO LIST

MY MOODS

FOR TOMORROW

QUICK NOTE

TO DO LIST

HEALTH & FITNESS

WATER INTAKE

TODAY'S NOTES

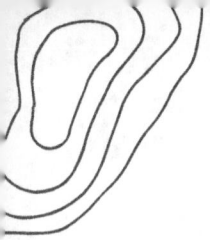
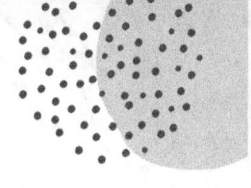

GOOD MORNING!!

___/___/___

M T W T F S S
○ ○ ○ ○ ○ ○ ○

TODAY'S APPOINTMENTS

6:00	7:00	8:00	9:00	10:00	11:00	12:00 PM	1:00	2:00	3:00	4:00	5:00	6:00

TO DO LIST

MY MOODS

FOR TOMORROW

QUICK NOTE

WATER INTAKE

TO DO LIST

HEALTH & FITNESS

TODAY'S NOTES

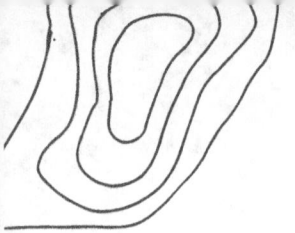

GOOD MORNING!!

___/___/___

M T W T F S S
○ ○ ○ ○ ○ ○ ○

TODAY'S APPOINTMENTS

6:00	7:00	8:00	9:00	10:00	11:00	12:00 PM	1:00	2:00	3:00	4:00	5:00	6:00

TO DO LIST

MY MOODS

FOR TOMORROW

QUICK NOTE

TO DO LIST

HEALTH & FITNESS

WATER INTAKE

TODAY'S NOTES

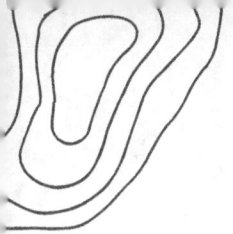

GOOD MORNING!!

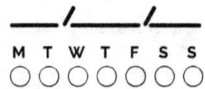

M T W T F S S
◯ ◯ ◯ ◯ ◯ ◯ ◯

TODAY'S APPOINTMENTS

6:00	7:00	8:00	9:00	10:00	11:00	12:00 PM	1:00	2:00	3:00	4:00	5:00	6:00

TO DO LIST

MY MOODS

FOR TOMORROW

QUICK NOTE

TO DO LIST

HEALTH & FITNESS

WATER INTAKE

TODAY'S NOTES

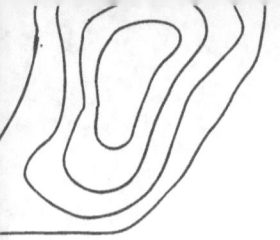

GOOD MORNING!!

____/____/____

M T W T F S S
○ ○ ○ ○ ○ ○ ○

TODAY'S APPOINTMENTS

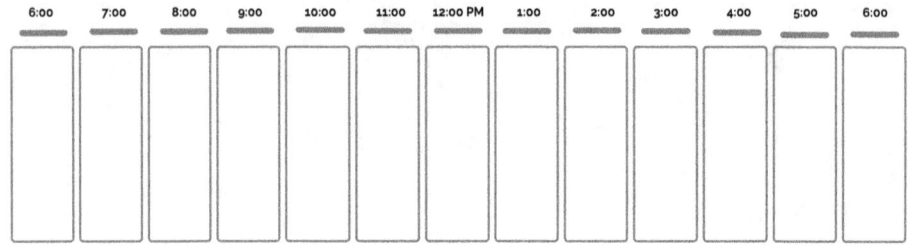

6:00	7:00	8:00	9:00	10:00	11:00	12:00 PM	1:00	2:00	3:00	4:00	5:00	6:00

TO DO LIST

MY MOODS

FOR TOMORROW

QUICK NOTE

TO DO LIST

HEALTH & FITNESS

WATER INTAKE

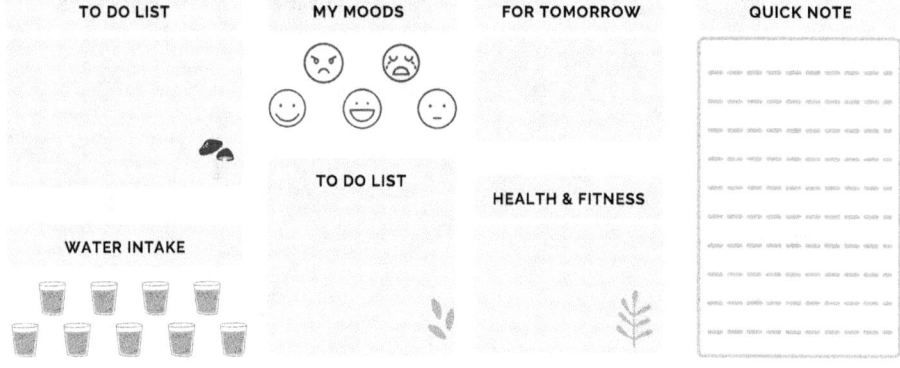

TODAY'S NOTES

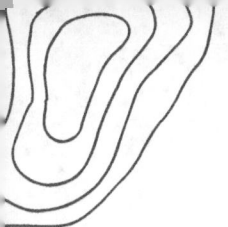

GooD MorNING!!

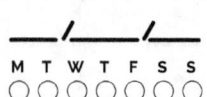

___/___/___

M T W T F S S
○ ○ ○ ○ ○ ○ ○

TODAY'S APPOINTMENTS

6:00	7:00	8:00	9:00	10:00	11:00	12:00 PM	1:00	2:00	3:00	4:00	5:00	6:00

TO DO LIST

MY MOODS

FOR TOMORROW

QUICK NOTE

TO DO LIST

HEALTH & FITNESS

WATER INTAKE

TODAY'S NOTES

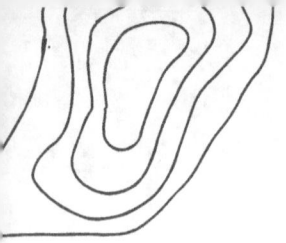

GOOD MORNING!!

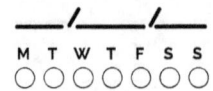

___/___/___

M T W T F S S
○ ○ ○ ○ ○ ○ ○

TODAY'S APPOINTMENTS

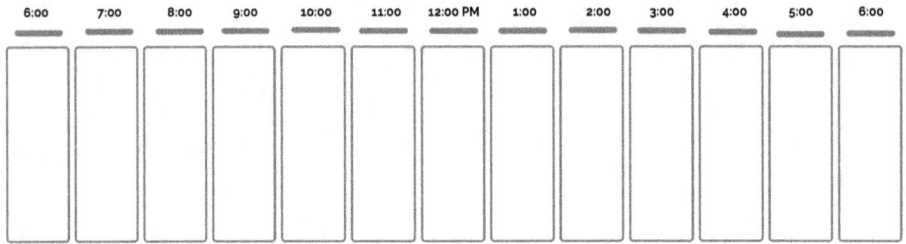

6:00	7:00	8:00	9:00	10:00	11:00	12:00 PM	1:00	2:00	3:00	4:00	5:00	6:00

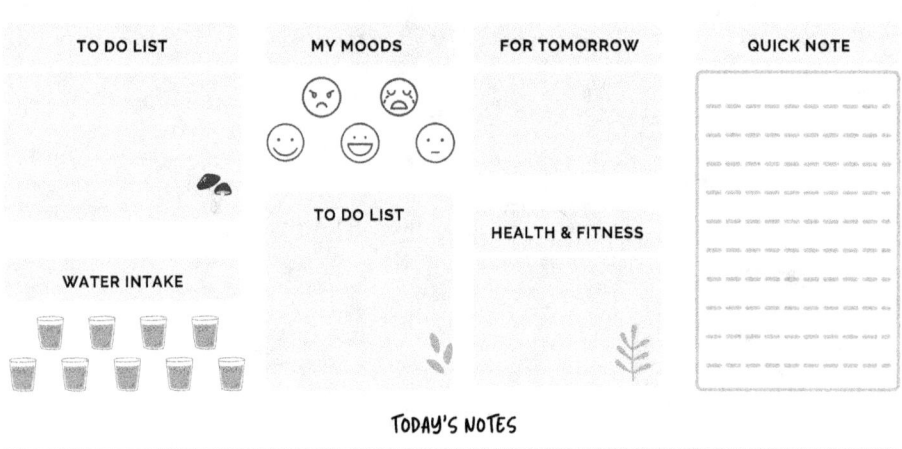

TO DO LIST

MY MOODS

FOR TOMORROW

QUICK NOTE

TO DO LIST

WATER INTAKE

HEALTH & FITNESS

TODAY'S NOTES

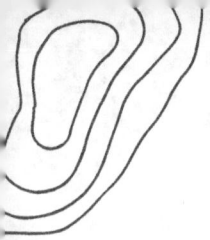
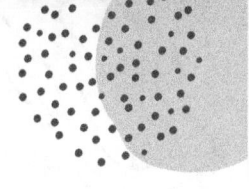

GooD MorNinG!!

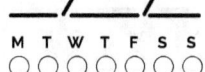

M T W T F S S
◯ ◯ ◯ ◯ ◯ ◯ ◯

TODAY'S APPOINTMENTS

6:00	7:00	8:00	9:00	10:00	11:00	12:00 PM	1:00	2:00	3:00	4:00	5:00	6:00

TO DO LIST

MY MOODS

FOR TOMORROW

QUICK NOTE

TO DO LIST

HEALTH & FITNESS

WATER INTAKE

TODAY'S NOTES

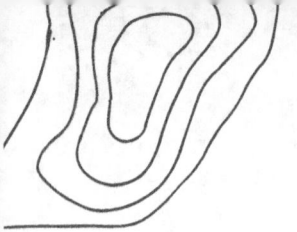

GOOD MORNING!!

___/___/___

M T W T F S S
○ ○ ○ ○ ○ ○ ○

TODAY'S APPOINTMENTS

6:00	7:00	8:00	9:00	10:00	11:00	12:00 PM	1:00	2:00	3:00	4:00	5:00	6:00

TO DO LIST

MY MOODS

FOR TOMORROW

QUICK NOTE

TO DO LIST

HEALTH & FITNESS

WATER INTAKE

TODAY'S NOTES

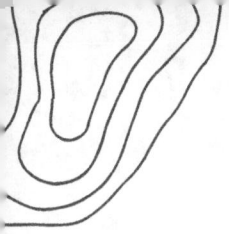

Good Morning!!

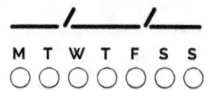

M T W T F S S
○ ○ ○ ○ ○ ○ ○

TODAY'S APPOINTMENTS

6:00	7:00	8:00	9:00	10:00	11:00	12:00 PM	1:00	2:00	3:00	4:00	5:00	6:00

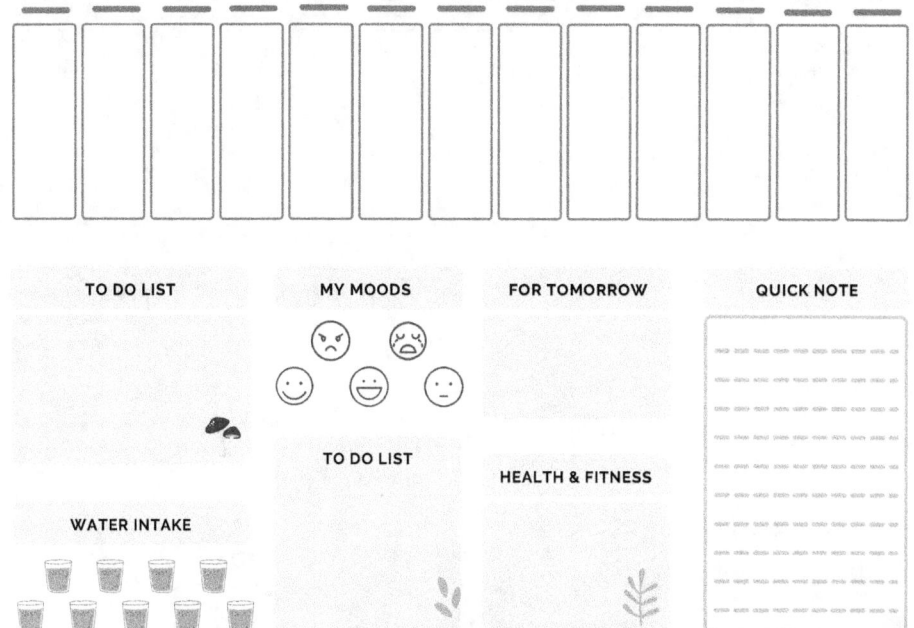

TO DO LIST

MY MOODS

FOR TOMORROW

QUICK NOTE

TO DO LIST

HEALTH & FITNESS

WATER INTAKE

TODAY'S NOTES

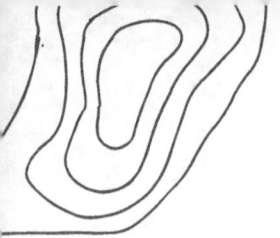

GOOD MORNING!!

___/___/___

M T W T F S S
○ ○ ○ ○ ○ ○ ○

TODAY'S APPOINTMENTS

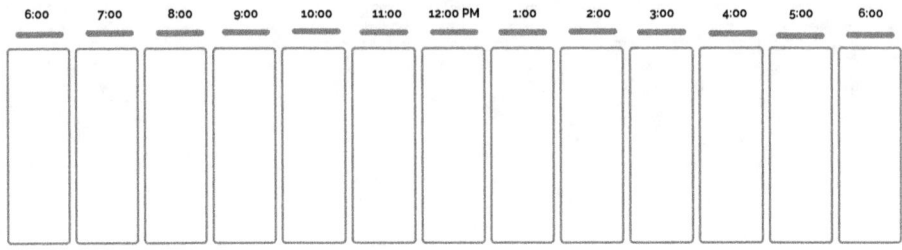

6:00	7:00	8:00	9:00	10:00	11:00	12:00 PM	1:00	2:00	3:00	4:00	5:00	6:00

TO DO LIST

MY MOODS

FOR TOMORROW

QUICK NOTE

TO DO LIST

HEALTH & FITNESS

WATER INTAKE

TODAY'S NOTES

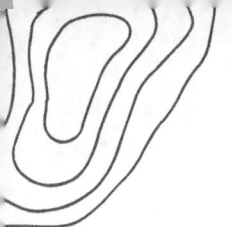

Good Morning!!

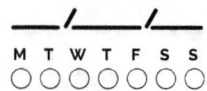

M T W T F S S
○ ○ ○ ○ ○ ○ ○

TODAY'S APPOINTMENTS

6:00	7:00	8:00	9:00	10:00	11:00	12:00 PM	1:00	2:00	3:00	4:00	5:00	6:00

TO DO LIST

MY MOODS

FOR TOMORROW

QUICK NOTE

TO DO LIST

HEALTH & FITNESS

WATER INTAKE

TODAY'S NOTES

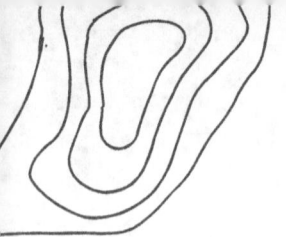

GOOD MORNING!!

___/___/___

M T W T F S S
○ ○ ○ ○ ○ ○ ○

TODAY'S APPOINTMENTS

6:00	7:00	8:00	9:00	10:00	11:00	12:00 PM	1:00	2:00	3:00	4:00	5:00	6:00

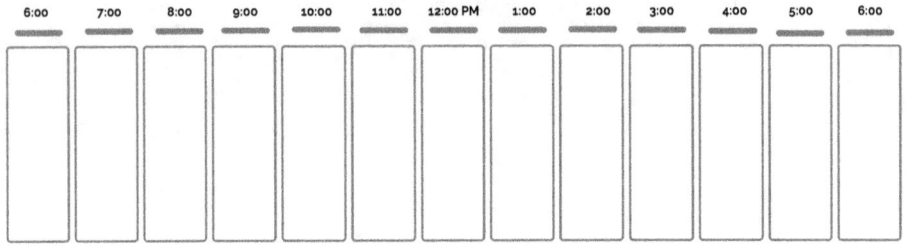

TO DO LIST

MY MOODS

FOR TOMORROW

QUICK NOTE

TO DO LIST

HEALTH & FITNESS

WATER INTAKE

TODAY'S NOTES

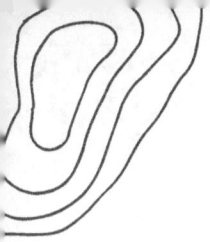
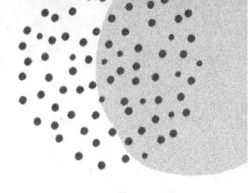

Good Morning!!

___/___/___

M T W T F S S
○ ○ ○ ○ ○ ○ ○

TODAY'S APPOINTMENTS

6:00	7:00	8:00	9:00	10:00	11:00	12:00 PM	1:00	2:00	3:00	4:00	5:00	6:00

TO DO LIST

MY MOODS

FOR TOMORROW

QUICK NOTE

TO DO LIST

HEALTH & FITNESS

WATER INTAKE

TODAY'S NOTES

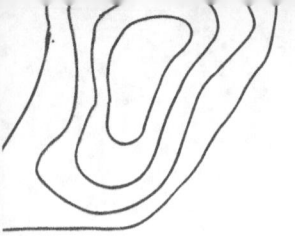

Good Morning!!

__/__/__

M T W T F S S
○ ○ ○ ○ ○ ○ ○

TODAY'S APPOINTMENTS

6:00	7:00	8:00	9:00	10:00	11:00	12:00 PM	1:00	2:00	3:00	4:00	5:00	6:00

TO DO LIST

MY MOODS

FOR TOMORROW

QUICK NOTE

TO DO LIST

WATER INTAKE

HEALTH & FITNESS

Today's Notes

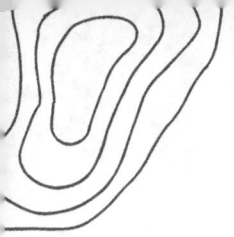
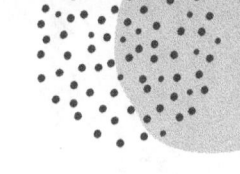

GOOD MORNING!!

___/___/___

M T W T F S S
○ ○ ○ ○ ○ ○ ○

TODAY'S APPOINTMENTS

6:00	7:00	8:00	9:00	10:00	11:00	12:00 PM	1:00	2:00	3:00	4:00	5:00	6:00

TO DO LIST

MY MOODS

FOR TOMORROW

QUICK NOTE

TO DO LIST

WATER INTAKE

HEALTH & FITNESS

TODAY'S NOTES

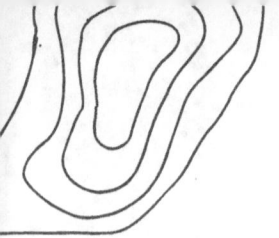

Good Morning!!

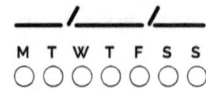

M T W T F S S
○ ○ ○ ○ ○ ○ ○

TODAY'S APPOINTMENTS

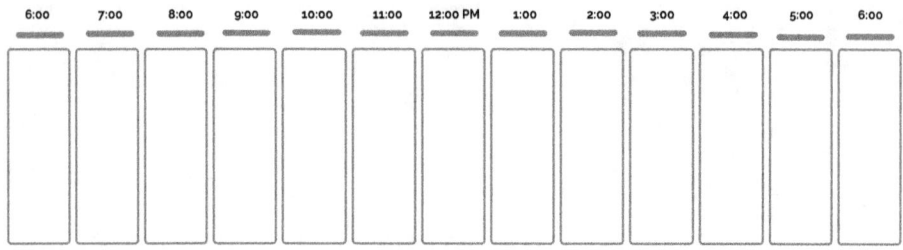

6:00	7:00	8:00	9:00	10:00	11:00	12:00 PM	1:00	2:00	3:00	4:00	5:00	6:00

TO DO LIST

MY MOODS

FOR TOMORROW

QUICK NOTE

TO DO LIST

HEALTH & FITNESS

WATER INTAKE

TODAY'S NOTES

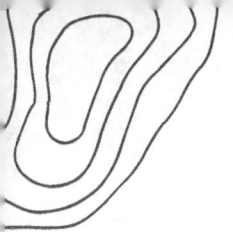

GOOD MORNING!!

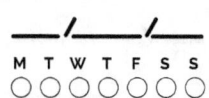

M T W T F S S
○ ○ ○ ○ ○ ○ ○

TODAY'S APPOINTMENTS

6:00	7:00	8:00	9:00	10:00	11:00	12:00 PM	1:00	2:00	3:00	4:00	5:00	6:00

TO DO LIST

MY MOODS

FOR TOMORROW

QUICK NOTE

TO DO LIST

HEALTH & FITNESS

WATER INTAKE

TODAY'S NOTES

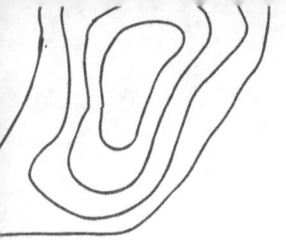

GOOD MORNING!!

___/___/___

M T W T F S S
◯ ◯ ◯ ◯ ◯ ◯ ◯

TODAY'S APPOINTMENTS

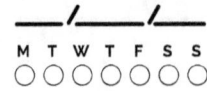

6:00	7:00	8:00	9:00	10:00	11:00	12:00 PM	1:00	2:00	3:00	4:00	5:00	6:00

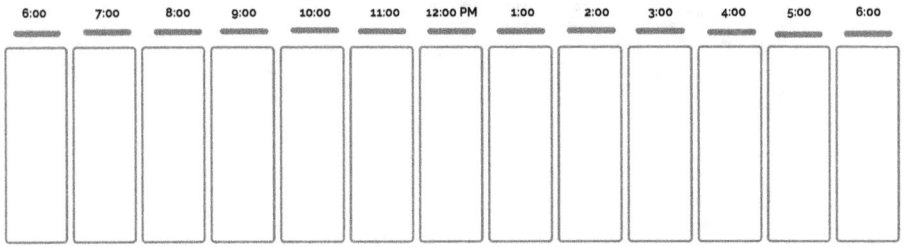

TO DO LIST

MY MOODS

FOR TOMORROW

QUICK NOTE

TO DO LIST

HEALTH & FITNESS

WATER INTAKE

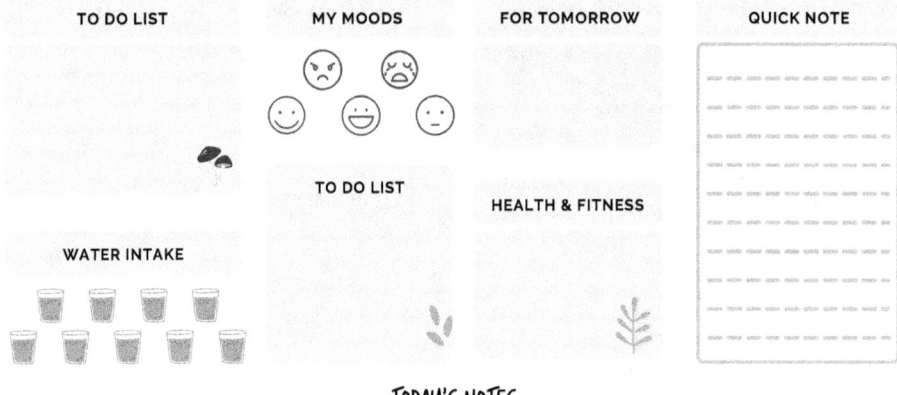

TODAY'S NOTES

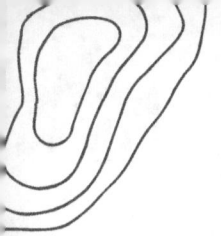
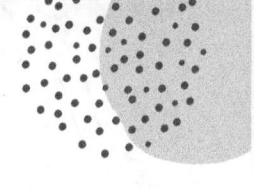

GOOD MORNING!!

___ / ___ / ___

M T W T F S S
○ ○ ○ ○ ○ ○ ○

TODAY'S APPOINTMENTS

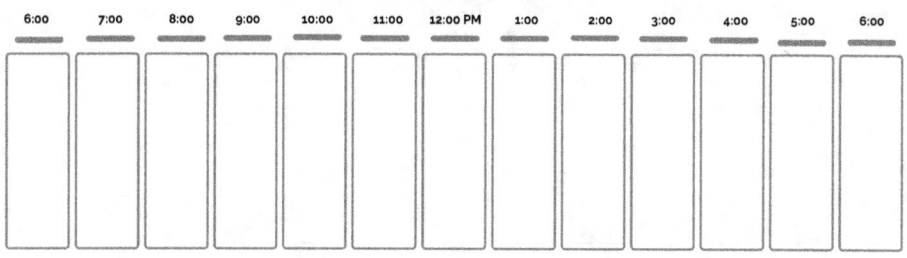

6:00	7:00	8:00	9:00	10:00	11:00	12:00 PM	1:00	2:00	3:00	4:00	5:00	6:00

TO DO LIST

MY MOODS

FOR TOMORROW

QUICK NOTE

TO DO LIST

HEALTH & FITNESS

WATER INTAKE

TODAY'S NOTES

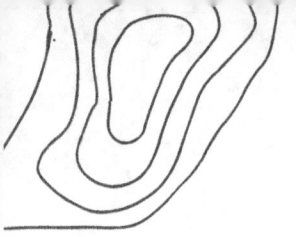

GOOD MORNING!!

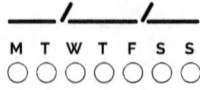

M T W T F S S
○ ○ ○ ○ ○ ○ ○

TODAY'S APPOINTMENTS

6:00	7:00	8:00	9:00	10:00	11:00	12:00 PM	1:00	2:00	3:00	4:00	5:00	6:00

TO DO LIST

MY MOODS

FOR TOMORROW

QUICK NOTE

WATER INTAKE

TO DO LIST

HEALTH & FITNESS

TODAY'S NOTES

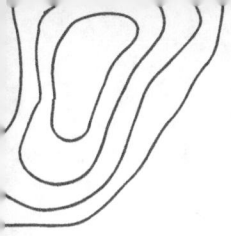

GOOD MORNING!!

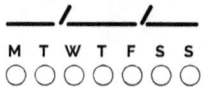

M T W T F S S
○ ○ ○ ○ ○ ○ ○

TODAY'S APPOINTMENTS

6:00	7:00	8:00	9:00	10:00	11:00	12:00 PM	1:00	2:00	3:00	4:00	5:00	6:00

TO DO LIST

MY MOODS

FOR TOMORROW

QUICK NOTE

TO DO LIST

HEALTH & FITNESS

WATER INTAKE

TODAY'S NOTES

HAVE A GREAT DAY!!

RE-ORDER

WWW.THE JOURNALBOX.COM

sales@thejournalbox.com | 215-298-9475

The Journal Box is a Woman, Minority & Veteran Owned Company

@2021 - The Journal Box